AF260801

# ESCAPE!

*Englishman takes family to America
in 1635 for religious freedom*

Meredith Platt

ISBN: 978-1-971940-16-8 (sc)
ISBN: 978-1-971940-17-5 (e)

Rev. date: 05/14/2026

# DEDICATION

THIS BOOK IS DEDICATED WITH LOVE,
PRIDE, AND GRATITUDE
TO MY FATHER:
CHAUNCEY LEEDS MITCHELL JR.

# ACKNOWLEDGMENT

I WOULD LIKE TO EXPRESS my
deep thanks to
David Glover, President
of the Halifax Antiquarian Society

David not only took us on an illuminating tour of the Minster but also introduced us to many of Matthew Mitchell's church contemporaries via the carvings on the walls of Coley Chapel, located closer to where Matthew and his family lived. Coley was Matthew's local parish church. David also drove us through the locale where the family most likely lived. He was most helpful and a fountain of information. His activities in the Society are most tempting . . . if on one the "Pond" weren't so big!

. . . TO MY HUSBAND, DAVID PIERSON:
ALL MY LOVE AND GRATITUDE. COULDN'T
HAVE HAPPENED WITHOUT YOU. YOU ARE
MY SAVANT AND MY CHEF.

# PREFACE

When I was growing up, every member of my family knew about my ancestors, especially Matthew. That is, we knew the overall story—how the  whole family came on a ship from England to America in 1635 to escape religious persecution. It was considered amazing not only that they all arrived alive but also that they all grew to adulthood and had healthy, successful lives.

My mother, Ann Mitchell, was the storyteller. Every night, she would read us either a fairy tale of our choice from the *Book of Knowledge* (1904 version of the children's *Encyclopedia Britannica*, which I still have) or read from *Matthew's Genealogy*, supplied by my father. We girls pushed for "The Twelve Dancing Princesses" while my brother urged, "How the Indians burned down Matthew's house."

My mother, an artist, had even painted the family crest which hung over the fireplace. My father would explain that the three seashells represented members of the family who had made crusades to the sea, "considered a noble deed."

Both stories were emotionally exciting and "true" as far as we were concerned. Of course, by the time we were adults, many histories had been written about the people who crossed the ocean to New England, and many of the details differed from one version to another. There is enough information now, however, so I could reconcile discrepancies to a satisfactory degree.

**When I was in my forties, married with a son, and attending Hunter College at night, my father pulled a large black box out of a closet and said he wanted to talk to me about it. The box was puzzling: it was made from heavy wood. It was too heavy to be a suitcase, but it had three initials on it:** N-M-S. These stood for Natalie Mitchell Seth, my father's aunt.

He opened it to reveal many turn-of-the-century photographs of relatives, unfortunately without names written on the back, and several hundred pages of beautifully cursive writing. He showed me the first page and told me it was Matthew Mitchell's genealogy. Compiled by aunts and uncles since 1905, it was updated each year and kept in the trunk. Every year, a group of Mitchells would meet at Natalie's house on Long Island to celebrate the anniversary of Matthew's arrival in America. New contributions to the genealogy would be read and discussed. The final meeting of the group was held in 1942. Due to the war, no one had enough gasoline ration stamps to drive to Long Island.

My father was told to hold onto the material until the end of the war when fuel was presumed to be available again, and the genealogy could be completed appropriately and perhaps published. It wasn't opened again until the day my father gave it to me. He said he was giving it to me because no one else in the family was interested in it. I was unable to work on it until I had completed my bachelor's degree and PhD. He understood.

When I did look at it, I was definitely impressed. In general, it was very high quality. The cursive writing was 100 percent legible. In today's world, particularly in public schools, children are no longer taught cursive writing. They are handed a computer at the front door. Many high school students cannot even sign their own names.

Natalie made a contribution of her own: she drew a "Family Tree" with a huge trunk. Matthew's name is on the trunk, and all the ancestor names climb up the tree. I will include a partial copy here.

By the time I wrote Matthew's story, I was definitely emotionally involved. I was cheering the whole family on and cursing the evildoers. I was happy to have dug up so much information about the trip itself and the passengers' resilience.

I hope you are prompted to find information about at least one of your ancestors that you can share with others. A Greek philosopher once said, "What you leave behind is not what is engraved on your tombstone, but what is woven into the lives of others."

# THE FAMILY TREE

Aunt Natalie Mitchell decided to contribute a Family Tree in the style of the day (1939). It is too large a tree to print in this book, but this will give you an idea of her effort. Matthew is the trunk, of course, and all the offspring grow out the branches. The enlargement of the upper right corner shows three Chaunceys (my grandfather, father, and brother), myself (Meredith), and my mother (Ann). Although my sister (Alexandra) was born a year before me, Natalie had not yet worked her onto a branch.

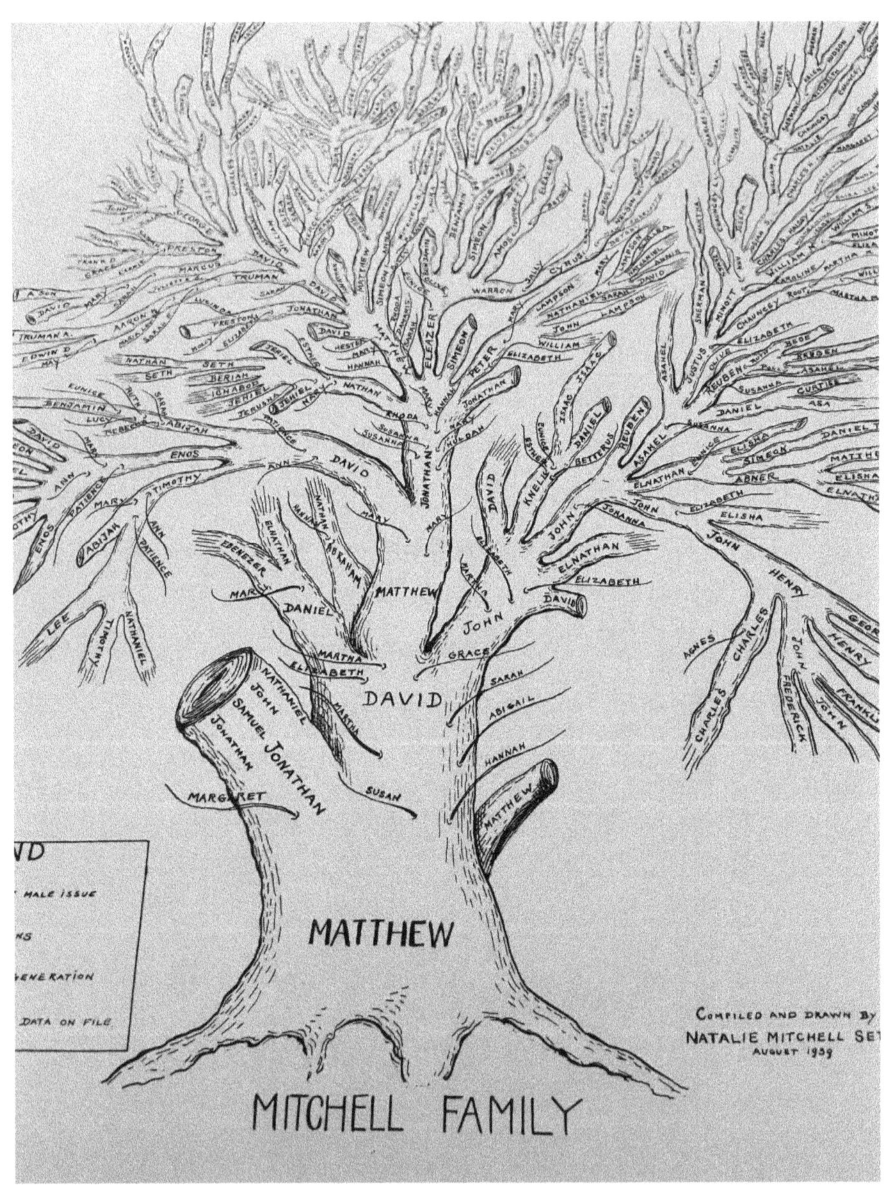

MITCHELL FAMILY
MATTHEW
DAVID
COMPILED AND DRAWN BY
NATALIE MITCHELL SE
AUGUST 1959
MALE ISSUE
GENERATION
DATA ON FILE

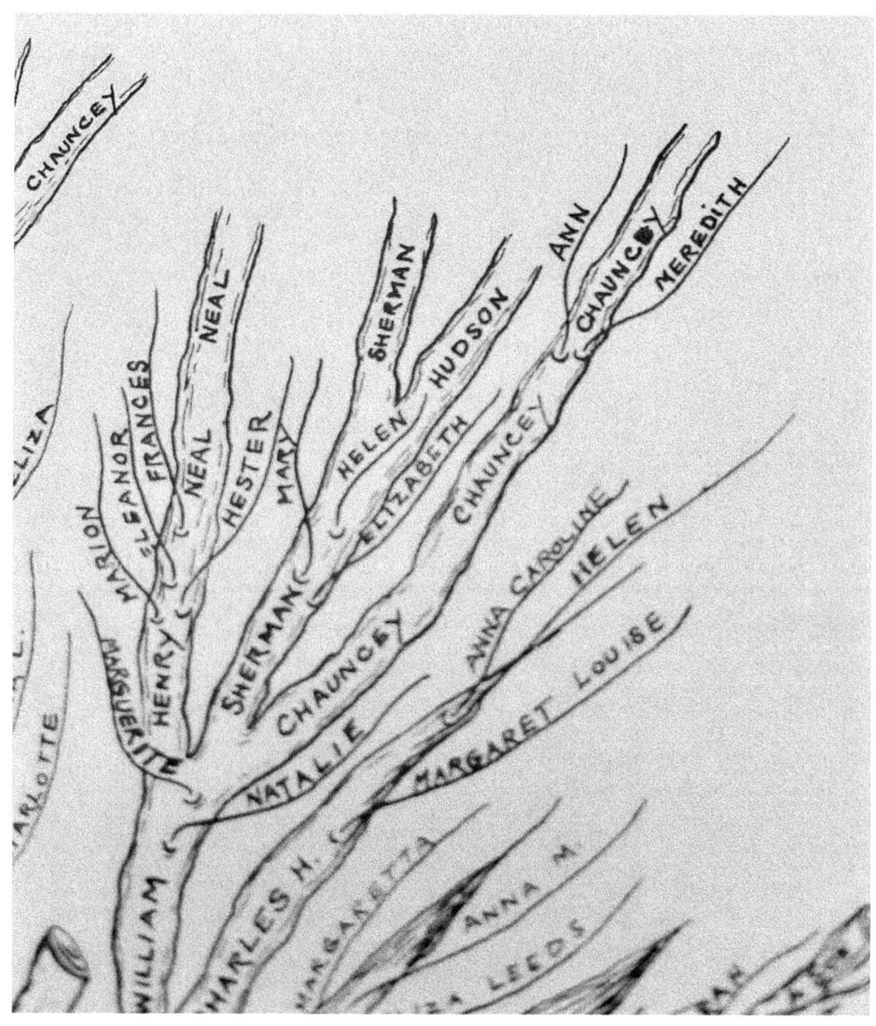

CHAUNCEY
NEAL
NEAL
SHERMAN
HUDSON
ANN
CHAUNCEY
MEREDITH
FRANCES
ELEANOR
HESTER
MARY
HELEN
ELIZABETH
CHAUNCEY
MARION
ELIZA
HENRY
SHERMAN
CHAUNCEY
ANNA CAROLINE
HELEN
MARGUERITE
NATALIE
MARGARET
LOUISE
CHARLOTTE
WILLIAM
CHARLES H.
MARGARETTA
ANNA M.
LEEDS

# MATTHEW MITCHELL'S GIFT

## BY MEREDITH PLATT

"A people who take no pride in the noble achievement of remote ancestors will never achieve anything worthy to be remembered with pride by remote descendants."

Macaulay: *History of England*

# THE OLD COUNTRY

Of all my ancestors, Matthew Mitchell was the best known in my family.  Although I've known about him all my life, I have no idea what he actually looked like.  No pictures are available. He lived the average life span for the time, fifty-five years, but his moment to shine in history spanned about ten years.

Matthew brought his family to America for religious freedom, and well, he should have. When he was born in 1590, most citizens were Catholic, which was the queen's religion, Elizabeth I. When she died in 1603, the new king, James I, was head of the Anglican Church. James strongly adhered to the Protestant faith, and his era became a time of renewed religious fervor. He expected all citizens to embrace the Protestant religion.

Puritans (who became known as Pilgrims) also flourished in the country at that time and, before James, had been tolerated. But now, they had high hopes that James would purify the Church of England by extinguishing all its Catholic roots. All churches were ordered to remove altar candles, flowers, statues, vestments, incense, and any rituals associated with the Catholic religion.

This process of change did not happen overnight. Many churches continued to function as before until physically forced by church authorities to stop. While Matthew was growing up, his church was relatively undisturbed. It was a quiet, warm, candlelit place.  He learned the prayers from his Catholic prayer book and followed the instructions of the minister. And when he had his own children, he taught them the same.

But religion became a big political issue. Being the wrong religion in one's community or church could get you imprisoned, tortured, or executed. Matthew remained a member of the Church of England.  However, he was seriously worried about being arrested for some infraction of all the new laws that were being established. In America, he believed, his congregation could determine its own affairs. In America, everyone in a particular area was assigned to the parish church, and each local parish submitted to the oversight of the larger church hierarchy.

Matthew was forty-five years old when I first "saw" him. This was on my first trip, in 2017, to Halifax, West Yorkshire, about a three-hour train ride north of London.  I was visiting the Halifax Minster, the Protestant Cathedral parish that has served the people of that city and surrounding towns for centuries and was Matthew's family parish.  I also wanted to see if the Mitchell family crest was painted on the church sanctuary ceiling, along with other local crests of the time, as suggested in the materials given to me by my father. While there is little doubt that I am descended from Matthew Mitchell, the authenticity of the crest is another matter.

David Glover, the church historian, genealogist, and willing searcher for ancestors, met my husband and me at the Halifax railroad station. Through my travel agent, I had arranged for him to spend two days with us, exploring the church and the area where Matthew and his family might have lived. David was a fountain of information and an endlessly patient listener to all my questions. He had arranged for us to tour a house built in the seventeenth century and to drive the countryside where Matthew most likely lived. Even the hotel he recommended dated from the seventeenth century.

We also spent several hours in the Halifax Minster Church, during which David "introduced" us to the pastors and primary church characters of Matthew's time, as depicted in paintings and carvings. We could touch the large baptismal font at the rear of the church where Matthew was baptized. The font has an ornate metal lid suspended over it that can be raised to the ceiling or lowered on top of the font as protection. It seems that during certain eras, it was a popular activity for parishioners to steal holy water.

I sat for a long time on a chair in the sanctuary, gazing up at the crests that had been painted on the ceiling. About twenty of them were said to be from Matthew's time and village. David had warned me that I would probably not recognize my own family's because all the paintings were blackened with the dirt of centuries. Apparently, they had been "cleaned" in the early 1940s but not "restored." Making matters worse, the church provided no lighting at the ceiling level. They were there, all right, but it was like looking for them in a black cave. The Halifax Minster, like all famous centuries-old cathedrals of the world, requires periodic restoration of the *whole* church, costing an enormous amount of money, which this parish did not have. Parts had been done, but not this part. So unless I could come up with at least $30,000, plus more for lighting, I would never be able to see a restored version of "our" painting.

I sat, looking up, for a long time. It felt sad. In other parts of the church, David had pointed out particular chapels, describing how they had looked when the church was built, how they had changed, and the role historical events played in those changes. For example, some changes reflect political/religious changes—such as allowing candles, flowers, incense, and ornate vestments, which can make a chapel feel warm and intimate. Other changes can create a cold and intimidating environment. In other cases, only a "ruin" remains, a ruin of a religion and a way of life.

In Matthew's adult years, the embracing church of his youth was long gone, the king had declared himself pope, and penalties were harsh for not complying with myriad rules of church attendance and payment for what was considered infractions of these rules. I thought of Matthew and all the others in Halifax, living through those times of enormous religious tumult, so threatening that thousands felt they could no longer live in England. They felt their lives depended upon escape. Many did . . . including Matthew.

From my twenty-first-century perch in the sanctuary of the Halifax Minster, I wanted to run out and win a big lottery! Immediately! I would hand all the money to David Glover and say, "Let's get started!"

But first, I must get to know Matthew and his family. In March of 1635, the family lived in a neighboring community called Southowram, a village that stands on a hilltop to the east of Halifax. A small Protestant church there, called Coley Chapel, is part of the Halifax Minster. This is the church where the Mitchells worshipped each Sunday. The pastor was the Rev. Richard Denton.

Matthew left Coley chapel one spring Sunday in 1635 and headed home at a brisk pace. Home was about four miles away, but he relished the walk. The day was sunny and warm, with a pleasant breeze.  He was excited, and his brain was still whirling from his latest conversation with the Reverend Denton. Denton has been his friend and spiritual advisor for years, and Matthew relied on his wisdom and advice. He always discussed the big decisions in his life with him first. Denton was a patient, uncritical listener, which contributed to his skill as a minister and preacher. His sermons were widely known and praised.

Matthew, by contrast, was neither patient nor uncritical. In fact, he could be quite argumentative. His ideas and opinions needed to be first voiced and tested in a "safe" environment. As a result, their conversations usually lasted for several hours, which this one did. (Matthew's wife and children were used to heading home from church far ahead and did not expect him for hours.)

Fortunately, over the years, Matthew learned to think before he spoke to the point that he was now welcomed in town meetings. He was considered a worthy candidate for committee posts and was an entertaining guest at parties. He was also a smart, practical thinker and a good problem solver. "And this is the biggest decision I've ever made," he told himself out loud, taking a deep breath.

As he reached the bottom of the steep hill, he headed across a wide meadow and began walking at a slower pace. Though not quite as burly as he had been at twenty-five, Matthew was still handsome and healthy, with flashing brown eyes and very dark brown, wavy hair. He had spent twenty years learning to make a living as a merchant and farmer, buying and selling everything—land, sheep, wool, houses, vegetables. Very enterprising, he was also cautious and meticulously honest. He did not like to be cheated, nor did he cheat others. As a result, he was trusted in the community and had saved quite a bit of money while living modestly.

Matthew's family was usual for his time: In seventeenth-century rural England, having a large family was a major asset. Sons helped work the farm, build the house, tended the animals, chopped wood for the fire, and generally did the heavy work. They also bore arms and protected the family in times of trouble. And these were perilous times right now in England. Civil war was looming. Older sons David and Jonathan were well trained in the use of guns and had military experience in their town militia.

Daughters were essential for cooking, cleaning, planting, and maintaining a kitchen garden for family food while helping their mother make clothing and helping to care for younger children, teaching them all they should know. The importance of their responsibilities cannot be minimized.

They were not just taught to "behave themselves." Their responsibilities helped keep the family safe. By misbehaving, they risked the lives of everyone in the family.

Creating and maintaining a family was a risky business. Death rates among infants and young children were high. Childbirth was dangerous, and there were no medications for the myriad illnesses contracted in a child's early years. Couples knew they might lose many of the children they created. Husbands died at an early age, and healthy widows of childbearing age did not stay single long.

For example, Susan Wood was married at eighteen and had one child when her husband, John Butterfield, died. That child lived with the Butterfield family. But Susan was a beautiful woman with dark blond hair, and she attracted young men. Two years later, she and Matthew married in the Halifax Minster. They raised eight healthy children. All of them would live to adulthood and raise their own families. All eight, as well as Matthew himself, were baptized in the large, marble baptismal font that still stands today, as it did then, in the rear of the Minster. I felt a real kinship with them all on the day I laid my two hands on that font.

Susan was not only hardworking but also artistic and clever. To provide clothing for her large family, she developed a business making and repairing clothing. The women have what they called a "clothing chain." They saved the smallest clothes and passed them on to a new mother nearby. All other children's clothing was cleaned, repaired, and organized in age-appropriate piles, which

Susan passed on to mothers who needed them. There was no monetary cost to anyone.

But Susan also collected the cast-off clothing of adults, and this is how she earned money. She was a very skilled seamstress, so she repaired, remade, altered, and cleaned this clothing to sell it. Women who worked as servants for the wealthy frequently passed on clothing discarded by their employers. Susan was willing to pay for these because she considered them "treasures." They were a source of delicate fabrics (such as velvets and silks), trimmings (lace, linens, and braids), and bright colors. The adult clothes were usually in better condition than the children's. Susan discarded nothing. Even the smallest pieces of fabric or trim could be used to enhance a little girl's dress or trim a collar on a woman's blouse. She learned how to set prices for each piece, depending upon the complexity of the design and the amount of trimming (and for whom she was creating it).

Over the years, her sewing talents became known in the Halifax area. Susan was the go-to person people came to for everyday and special-occasion clothing. She gave Matthew most of her earnings because she knew how important it was for their daily living. But a percentage she held back, putting it in a secret place (not secret to Matthew, though) as savings for some future need or family wish. And by now, she, like Matthew, had accumulated a tidy sum.

Matthew was calmer now as he started up the next slope toward home. Only two more miles. Three of his children were now teenagers, two of them girls. They all had important afternoon jobs helping their mother. During the mornings, Susan taught reading and writing to all the children who were old enough. The younger children were aged four, six, eight, eleven, and twelve. No more babies, thank the good Lord! In fact, Matthew and Susan thanked God every day that not one of these eight was snatched at an early age by illness. Just keeping them fed and warm had been a big job! The worst illness the family had experienced was Jonathan's case of the flu during an epidemic in the winter of his tenth year. A close call, but he survived.

Today, after many long talks, Matthew announced to the Reverend Denton that he had decided to take his family to America. Denton responded that he too wanted to go. Matthew said he planned to leave on one of the first ships in the spring or summer. Due to the turbulent religious and political climate all over England, thousands of people, with or without their families, had already emigrated, either to Holland or America. Those moving to Holland were called Separatists and generally believed their worship should be separate from a central church. Most, like Matthew, wanted to move for religious reasons, while others were strictly adventurers seeking money and land.

The period from about 1586 (four years before Matthew was born) until now (1635) had been the most volatile. "Separatists" did not support some of the fundamental principles of the Church of England (such as a hierarchy of clergy and the wearing of vestments). Many citizens disagreed with the Act of Uniformity that was passed, saying it was illegal not to attend the official Church of England services every Sunday and holy days and pay a one-shilling penalty for not attending.

"Dissenters" were various Protestant groups that refused to take communion in the Church of England and conform to the restored Church of England. Other penalties could land you in jail or even larger fines. James I enforced these punitive laws. These days, the king considered himself to be the head of the church. Thus, many people decided to move to Holland or America.

Matthew told Denton that he and Susan were becoming quite apprehensive. When Matthew was a child, his church was a quiet place where he could feel safe, protected by God and people they knew, lit by flickering candles and fragrant with the incense used during ceremonies. It was a refuge from the world and all its uncertainties.

Now, the world had intruded. Orders were issued saying no one may be Catholic and all must attend the Church of England every Sunday. Punishments were inflicted on those who did not obey. Everyone lived under the threat of being picked up by police and questioned.

A cousin of Susan's, for example, had been jailed for minor religious violations . . . minor, at least, in Matthew's mind, such as reading an unapproved prayer book during Sunday services. It was the kind of thing that stuck in Matthew's craw. "A new king is crowned, and suddenly, we can't read the Bible we've had since we were children!"

Denton always let Matthew vent his anger and then assured him that these new rules just signified a changing of the guard. "Many, many of our parishioners disagree with current church leadership," he said. "As you know, these people have declared themselves 'dissenters' and have emigrated to America where they believe they can practice their religion as they wish."

"Well, that's what I want to do!" Matthew retorted too loudly. "I'm a dissenter!"

"Well, I'm not sure you're a dissenter," answered Denton with a chuckle, "but you certainly aren't happy with what's going on."

Matthew knew the choice was not an easy one. He had been listening to the talk in Halifax about life in America, and from what people were saying, it was a fearsome choice. First of all, traveling across the ocean was a huge risk. Some ships were simply never heard of again. "What do I know about sailing? Nothing." Apparently, the natives are violent. Being brutally killed by Indians was a likely prospect. Some say there was no source of clean water and food, and diseases were plentiful. And that's just the beginning! But the chance to have freedom of religion still sounded attractive to Matthew. He longed for a return to the peaceful religion of his childhood.

"How will I tell the children?" he wondered as he headed up the last hill to his home. "What if they don't want to go?" He stopped walking and sat down on a rock. He needed their help, but, more importantly, he wanted them to have a life of opportunity and religious freedom. That's why he must take them all. *The only one I would consider leaving behind with relatives is Jonathan,* he thought. Jonathan had suffered so much and, in fact, had nearly died the previous winter. Matthew wondered if he could survive even the journey, much less the difficult life once they arrived. The high fevers of his illness had left his left arm bent and stiff. He could barely use it for any purpose. Would the strain of the journey be too much for him? He must talk more with Susan about this issue, he thought as he stood up and began walking again.

Generally speaking, he thought the children would be excited and happy at the prospect of sailing on a big ship with other families to a new place. Matthew would explain it to them in great detail . . . and warn them about discussing it with friends. On the other hand, Abigail and Sarah were teenagers and were very attached to their friends.

He could see his house now, so he picked up his pace. Susan knew his plan, so he was sure she would have all the children in the house anticipating a "family conversation." And so it appeared as he approached the front door: there wasn't a child in sight outside nor a single sound to be heard. He swung open the door to see Susan and all the children seated around the room, still as statues. Nine pairs of eyes were glued to him.

Four-year-old Hannah jumped up from her spot on the floor near the fire and ran to him. "Father, Father," she called out, hurling herself into his arms. Matthew picked her up and hugged her enthusiastically. The rest of the "statues" slowly came alive and greeted him. Susan remained seated in her chair, smiling at him as he moved toward her. Hannah jumped down and moved back to her spot by the fire as Matthew leaned down to give Susan a kiss and hug. He then sat down on the hearth and addressed them all.

"My family," he began, "sometimes, life brings adventure, and this family is about to go on a BIG adventure!"

The children all began to talk at once. "What adventure?" "Why, Father?" "What's happened?" they all chimed. Matthew raised his hand to quiet the din and began to speak.

"We are going to go on a ship to live in America! There, we will have a farm, and animals, and lots of land. America is very beautiful. Many people from here and all over England are there already. You will make new friends to play with, and we'll all work hard to make our new house beautiful. We will even have a church, and the Reverend Denton will come also. You can write letters to your friends in England about your new and exciting life."

"But, Father," said Sarah, who was fourteen, "why are we going? Will my friends come?"

Matthew was quiet for a moment, thinking carefully before he spoke. Hannah ran across the room and sat on her mother's lap. "We have been fortunate as you children have been growing. We once had a small dark house with only two rooms. We had only three small windows with shutters and a thatch roof. No matter what we did, we were cold and wet all winter. Now, we have a brick house with two stories! And *two* glass windows! The big fireplace gives us lots of heat, and the slate roof keeps out the rain. We have animals, a barn, and good land to raise our own food. So I can understand your question, Sarah.

"You older children have, no doubt, been hearing about the new king and the changes he wants to make in our religion. Well, those changes affect everything . . . the taxes we pay to the king, the prayer book we read in church, the clothes we must wear to church, where we can sit in church, and how we must behave in our communities. Some of these changes are small and do not affect our lives. But many people cannot accept some of the changes and will not. I, for one, think the new taxes are too high, and I do not want to pay them!

"America is a free land," he continued more quietly, "and our church fathers decided how we are to dress and what prayer book we can read . . . " Matthew realized suddenly that he was again beginning to speak loudly, so he stopped.

"Tell them about the ship, Matthew, and what they will do on the ship," said Susan. "Tell them what *you* will do on the ship." Matthew understood that Susan was giving him a chance to calm down so that he wouldn't frighten the children.

"Well," he said with a smile, "I don't know yet which ship we will be on, but it will be large. One hundred people can sail on her, plus the crew. And we will have cows on board, and sheep, and other animals. As soon as I know the name of the boat, I will tell you. Inside the ship are places for all of us to sleep. We will also take food to eat during the trip."

"How long will it take to get there, Father?" asked David.

"I don't know, exactly," Matthew replied. "Should be about six weeks. We'll be going during the summer, so the weather should be warm and pleasant. The wind must blow from the east and south so the sails can carry us in the right direction. None of us has ever sailed on the ocean before, so this will be very new for us. Perhaps some of the sailors can teach us about the ship . . . how to furl the lines, wash the decks . . . learn to talk like sailors! Blimey, they've practically got their own language!" He laughed, and the children did too, some of them imitating sailor talk.

Susan began to speak. "Now, we'll all have to help to get ready to depart. Most important will be the food. You girls can all help me with that," she said, patting little Hannah on her head. "Some food will be dried, some will be stored in pottery jars, and some will be wrapped. And we'll have to count everything and make a list! We'll need to be sure we have enough for the whole trip."

Matthew thought they had enough information for the first talk. "We'll talk together many times before we leave, and you'll be able to ask all the questions you want. If I don't know the answers right away, I'll find out. And David will help me!" he added, putting his arm around his older son.

"Sure, Dad," said David, surprisingly shaking his father's hand. "We'll get everything organized."

"Now, you children run outside and play," said Susan, putting Hannah down. "It's a beautiful day out there!"

The children all jumped up and ran out the front door, chattering to one another.

When the room emptied out except for the parents, Matthew heaved a big sigh, brought over the only other chair in the room, and sat down next to Susan. "You did very well," she said quietly. "That's about all they need to know for now."

"Well, it's not all *I* need to know," said Matthew. "So far, all I know is that we have to pay a hefty fee for the trip over and then a lot more during the first few years. And some people want to invest money but not even go! They just see it as a financial opportunity. They're only looking to get rich!"

Susan smiled. "As usual!" She added, "No doubt we're in for a lot of surprises." They were both quiet for a few minutes, just looking at the fire and thinking. Then Susan took both of Matthew's hands in hers and looked him in the eye. "Don't worry," she said. "We've faced things like this before. You'll be very careful and ask lots of questions. We'll look out for ourselves. And, in the end, if it looks too risky, we just won't go . . . But I think we can make it!"

As he went about his typical day, Matthew started making a mental list of all the topics he must research: *What ships will be going to America this spring and summer,*

Matthew's head was whirling by the time he returned home each night. He hardly knew where to start. One of the first things he did was discuss with his son, David, which port all the ships were departing from. Bristol was the nearest major port for Halifax and the one most used for transatlantic trips, but certainly, that was not close. It was 200 miles away, on the west coast of England! How would they all get there? The roads were not really roads but trails with muddy ruts, and there were no wagons made to transport people. Occasionally, you could locate a stagecoach running between major towns, but none large enough for his family. Also, stagecoaches were just being invented, were very expensive, and had no springs, guaranteeing they were *very* uncomfortable. And there was also the danger of highwaymen.

As a start, he would ask David to talk to all the people he knew, asking from where the ships embarked, writing down whatever ship names he could and any other information he could about the journey. They could discuss it each night. He, himself, would talk with Reverend Denton and get his advice on which ship to travel and what the dangers might be. And he had some more personal questions for Denton: Matthew owned considerable land. How can he carry (and keep) his money and deeds in a safe place if he sells his land? Must he carry it on his person at all times? He would also need to talk with Susan about this.

Matthew had an idea about how they might get to Bristol. He went to talk to his close friend and business partner, Stephen, who was frequently transporting hogsheads full of farm products for export. (Hogsheads were large barrels, forty-eight inches high and thirty inches in diameter, first used to transport and store tobacco and, later, many other products. Stephen had many heavy wagons. Matthew figured he might have something to suggest.

The two men talked privately for several hours, and Matthew came home feeling very encouraged . . . but also afraid. Stephen told him they must get to Bristol as soon as possible because all the people boarding the ships were under suspicion, and men were coming aboard each day to check their identity papers. He thought he could adapt a few of his carts to fit Matthew's family, but they must not discuss their conversation and plans with anyone. Travel to Bristol would take at least a week.

Next, Matthew went to see Reverend Denton. He started with the most practical question: "From whom do I buy the tickets?"

Denton heaved a sigh and slowly began, "There are many ways, and you must be careful. Some people will steal your money and give you nothing. And other people are well-meaning but don't have the connections to get you on the right ship at the right time.

"You should begin by learning about the companies that have formed to do this. For example, The Virginia Company has sponsored many ships full of people who are taken to Virginia to settle that area. A group of Puritans recently left aboard the *Mayflower*, but I haven't heard how that turned out. Then, there's the Massachusetts Bay Company, wanting to sponsor people going to New England. It was founded by a group of businessmen to trade in furs and other goods. William Pynchon, who is just about your age, is a leader of that company. His background is a little different, of course. He is the son of a country gentleman who owns houses and land near Chelmsford. He knows a lot about the whole process.

"Five years ago, Pynchon sold some of the land he inherited from his father and bought a share in the company for L25. This made him a shareholder and a leader who has helped run the company's affairs ever since. Some of those who sailed for the company also went for religious reasons, similar to you and me. Pynchon anticipated the religious strife and civil war in England sooner than we did and rushed to organize plans to emigrate. He not only took his wife and four children with him, but he also took several servants and workers (carpenters to build houses, for example). He anticipated the political situation sooner than we did.

"Once you get there, I suggest you look him up. He ran his family's plantation and seemed to know a lot about identifying good land. Whatever you do, don't give anyone any money until you are on board the ship and embarking. When you buy the tickets, you will probably be given a compact that you must sign at the time of boarding and hand to the ship's captain. That compact tells what you will get when you arrive (in terms of land, lodging, and food) and what you owe for this. Some agreements give you land but demand that you give all the profits from selling the food you raise to the company for five years."

Matthew gasped! *Five years!* He was counting on those first five years to secure and establish his family and their home. And if, for some reason, the ship didn't arrive until late in the summer, how would he get sufficient crops in the ground for the winter? Well, all right, he would do what Reverend Denton advised. One thing at a time . . .

A few days later, Matthew and his brother-in-law, Samuel Butterfield, sat in the local inn having a beer and talking over the plan. Samuel also wanted to take members of his family to America. He had heard a few horror stories about the colonists being swindled, so he was very wary. "Who pays for the ship and the provisions? How do the investors think they're going to get their money back?" asked Samuel.

"I spoke with a Mr. Weston, representing the Virginia

Company," answered Matthew. "They expect to not only get their money back but also to make a profit. They draw up a compact that everyone must sign when they board the ship. In exchange for our transportation and provisions for the winter, we would have to give our labor for five days a week for five years, harvesting crops, trapping furs, drying fish. The profits would be theirs. Two days a week, we could work for ourselves."

Samuel didn't respond right away. He gazed up thoughtfully at the ceiling and then said, "Be careful what you sign. They'll get everything you've got!" He had never heard of Pynchon. "I think we have to find out more about how people make out once they get to New England. How were the accommodations and food? How were the land parcels they were promised? I heard of a ship called the *Mayflower*. How did they make out?" The two men agreed to meet frequently to compare the information.

Soon, Matthew had information on the new London Company. Those men were currently administering New Netherland and the Hudson River area. What they wanted next was to administer the *whole* Hudson River area because the land was so fertile, and the animal skins were so plentiful. So they wrote a new grant saying that the Virginia government and the Hudson River area would be under their control. Even more, annual meetings of the board would be held in America, not England.

They knew they were competing with The Hudson's Bay Company as well as the Plymouth Council for New

England. However, they added a rule to the Hudson's Bay group: *At the end of their first seven years of working for the company, half of everything the immigrants had built (including their homes) or earned or settled reverts to the company investors.* Working two days a week for themselves was dropped from the compact.

"That's highway robbery!" said Samuel. "We'd never get through the first winter." So the two men kept gathering information, eliminating some prospects, and refining their criteria.

Matthew was becoming frantic. If they didn't sign on to a ship soon, they would miss the summer season and would have to wait until the following year. A lot could happen in a year. Meanwhile, another of his friends had been sent to jail. Then, one Sunday early in April, he got lucky. He overheard several friends talking about the Rev. Richard Mather. He had never met Mather but had heard that he was in trouble. Now, Mather was in Bristol, signed onto a ship. Andrew, a friend of Matthew's from Mather's church, was visiting in Halifax. Matthew rushed to see him, and he agreed to tell him the whole story. They met by the canal, where Andrew shared all he knew.

Mather was about the same age as Matthew, born near Liverpool. He studied at Winwick grammar school nearby. His education was harsh, including daily beatings by the schoolmaster. After this initial schooling, Richard moved to Toxteth Park, a suburb of Liverpool, where he lived with Edward Aspinwall. At the age of fifteen, he was asked to take charge of the school there. During this time, Mather converted to Puritanism. After three years, he took a position as a preacher at Toxteth Park. He was ordained in the Church of England in 1619, ordained a minister in 1620, and preached there until 1633 when he was suspended for nonconformity in matters of ceremony.

"Ha!" said Matthew. "That's the kind of trouble I'm always getting into. What did he do?"

"He never wore a surplice," said Andrew. Apparently desiring not to engage in the Puritan "sin of conformity," Richard Mather refused to wear the "surplice," a papal robe. He preached as he saw fit for at least ten years until he was finally silenced in 1633. He was briefly reinstated, then silenced again—permanently—in 1634. Now, he has decided to take his family to America.

"I want to meet him!" said Matthew with enthusiasm. "I would be happy to take my family on the same ship, and I think I could be of help to him. Can you introduce me?"

Andrew said Matthew would have to get to Bristol quickly and make the arrangements. He did not know when Mather's ship would be leaving, but it would be soon. And he must not discuss these plans with anyone. Andrew would give him a letter of introduction to Mather. The two men stood up, shook hands, and Matthew headed for home.

When Andrew and Mather finished talking, Matthew knew that a) he and Mather would like each other, b) he was downright scared by all hat Andrew told him, and c) he definitely wanted to go on this ship!  He told Andrew he would do all he could to support Mather during the trip, make sure his identity was protected, and care for all the animals.

Susan was enthusiastic about this new prospect but said they must make plans quickly. Since Bristol was so far away from Halifax, Matthew said he would arrange with a business friend to have carriages take the family there. "I have friends I can trust," Matthew said.

The next morning, Susan took Matthew and David aside and told them she was against six-year-old Matthew going on the trip. She had been up half the night thinking about the children and she'd made some decisions. "First of all, Matthew is only six. This is all going to be rough going, even after we get there. And, in addition, he just recovered from a very bad winter cold.

As you know, the younger the child, the more likely they are to die. I woke Abagail up early this morning to see how she felt about everything. She flat-out said she did not want to go. She said she could live with her aunt and uncle and be a big help to them. She said she had lots of friends, including boys. "In a few years, I could be married!"

"Would you be willing to take care of little Matthew?" "Sure," said Abagail. "And maybe Martha will want to stay and help. She's all into her friends, now that she's twelve. She could be a big help."

"How does that sound?" Susan said to Matthew.

Matthew stood in silence.  He was dumbfounded.  On

the one hand, it made him feel very sad to imagine being so far away from three of their children.  On the other hand, it was a perfect decision given the circumstances! He paced up and down in front of the fireplace while he thought.  The only one not accounted for was Jonathon.

The next morning, Susan took Matthew aside and said she'd been awake

half the night thinking about the children and she'd made some decisions.

"First of all, Matthew is only six. This is all going to be rough going, even after

we get there. And, in addition, he just recovered from a very bad winter cold.

As you know, the younger the child, the more likely they are to die. I woke Abagail up early this morning to see how she felt about everything. She flat-out said she did not want to go. She said she could live with her aunt and uncle and be a big help to them. She said she had lots of friends, including boys. "In a few years, I could be married!"

"Would you be willing to take care of little Matthew?" "Sure," said Abagail. "And maybe Martha will want to stay and help. She's all into her friends, now that she's twelve. She could be a big help."

"How does that sound?" Susan said to Matthew.

"And don't worry about Jonathon," said Susan with a smile,.  "I spoke to him already, and it's okay with me."

They would proceed with caution, Susan thought, telling

no one. She stood up, took the teapot from the stand in the fireplace, and poured them both a cup of tea. She did not want to rush this conversation.

Matthew leaned back in his chair and told her everything he learned from his friend Stephen, Reverend Denton, and his friend, Andrew. Then every so often, she would ask a question. "What is the name of the ship?" She asked.

"The *James*," Matthew replied.

"What kind of cart does Stephen have in mind?"

"Well," Matthew answered with a chuckle, "it won't be comfortable! He's taking his largest carts and putting in a bench along three sides. That will be room enough for all of us. He's going to cushion it but says it will still be pretty hard. There are no springs. Our belongings will be stowed on the floor and under the seats, or in a second cart if necessary! Then he's building a frame over the top with a canvas cover in case it rains. He will have his men do all the driving. All we have to do is survive! There are two or three inns along the way where we can stop overnight to change the horses and get a hot meal, and there is an inn in Bristol where we can stay until we actually board the ship."

"Well, it all sounds pretty good to me," Susan said with a smile, "not cozy, but doable." Then she sat on Matthew's lap and gave him a long hug. "You've done a great job!" she said with a smile. "Now, I have another matter to discuss."

She was worried about their six-year-old son, Matthew. David reported to her that little Matthew told him he did not want to go on the journey. He was afraid and wanted to stay at home in England. Every night, he would cry himself to sleep. Susan suggested that David tell him stories each night about sailing that all had happy endings. "David has been doing that, and it seems to help a little. But it still takes a long time to get him to sleep." Matthew said he would see what he and David could come up with. "Let's think about that," said Susan.

That afternoon, Matthew and David took the six-year-old for a walk to the canal not far from their home. They managed to go aboard one of the canal barges parked there. They were able to see the rooms below deck as well as the wheel, where the barge was steered, and storerooms for food and water. The little boy began to get interested in how a ship worked. David and Matthew decided to give themselves "sailor names" and asked the younger Matthew what he would like his to be. Little Matthew said he would like to be called "Barnacle" because that was a "tough" name.

"Right!" said his father. "That's a good one. I think I will be called 'Captain Mitch' because I'm the captain of our family. David, how about you?"

David thought for a minute. "How about 'Watcher,'" he said, "because I'm always watching out for you two?" Both Matthews laughed.

"That's great," said the father. "Now, we're all set. Let's go home and tell your mother and the rest of the family."

While the family was laughing and talking and making

up "sailor names" for themselves, Matthew's friend, Andrew, walked toward their house. Andrew said he knew that Richard Mather would want to meet him. Settling themselves around the fire, Andrew handed Matthew a long letter of introduction, carefully worded to reveal no incriminating information that he had written for Matthew to take with him. He was sure that Mather would welcome him and be very grateful for the help. He was also taking his own family, and they all had to remain incognito.

Mather had already had one perilous journey. On a ship he traveled from Warrington, he wrote in his log that the trip was "healthful," but he meant he had "escaped alive." Apparently, some men, known as "Searchers," came aboard before the ship left. They were looking for people attempting to escape prosecution by the church. They checked everyone's documents and asked questions. Fortunately, the Searchers signed off on them. However, Mather had to change his clothing and appearance daily for fear of being recognized. He was afraid this would be the case until he was well out to sea.

Mather had chosen the ship, the *James*, on which he wanted to sail with his parishioners. "He has spoken with the captain," said Andrew. "It's important that you all get there as soon as possible because she will depart once the winds are favorable. Some passengers for the *James* were already in Bristol, and others arrived after Mather. They boarded once, but the ship was not ready. Heaps of goods had not been stowed and were just lying in disordered piles here and there on the deck. The winds were favorable for sailing, but some people were already becoming seasick. The mariners insisted they could not go until everything was stowed and the hatches or decks above had been cleared. So they were all forced to give a hand with the goods."

Andrew said Matthew and his family should come aboard soon because when the winds changed, the ship would depart. Matthew said he and the family would go as quickly as possible and make arrangements with the captain. Andrew said Mather told him that the day he came aboard the *James*, "We found many diverse passengers and among them some loving and godly Christians who were glad to see us there."

The *James* was built primarily to carry cargo, with lots of room belowdecks. Although other ships often had guns to protect against pirates, this one did not but could hold up to 100 passengers plus the crew and had already made several trips to America carrying settlers. It had never been in a wreck, according to a sailor Andrew spoke with.

"She's yar!" said the sailor.

Andrew and Matthew talked for a long time that day. Andrew had one vital thing to tell him. "I heard what happened with the *Mayflower*," he said.

"Tell me everything. Was Mr. Pynchon on board?"

"No, he wasn't," said Matthew. "At the last minute, he switched to a sister ship in the fleet.

But a lot of people on the *Mayflower* were sick." Matthew had heard that conditions in the colonies were extremely difficult and many of them died during the winter. Promises made by companies were greatly exaggerated. Housing often consisted of a trench in the ground with a thatch roof. But that was five years ago. Hopefully, things would be better now.

When Andrew and Matthew finished talking, Matthew knew that a) he and Mather would like each other, b) he was downright scared by all that Andrew told him, and c) he definitely wanted to go on this ship! He told Andrew he would do all he could to support Mather during the trip, make sure his identity was protected, and care for all the animals. Matthew thanked Andrew. The two men shook hands, wished each other luck, and Andrew departed.

Susan, Matthew, and David talked late into the night. Susan was equally excited and apprehensive, but she trusted her husband in situations like this. David was likewise enthusiastic and promised to do whatever he could to help. He also reported to Matthew that he had carved a toy ship out of wood for "Barnacle." They would take it down to the canal to sail it, having some "high adventures."

Matthew took Susan aside the following morning and asked her how she felt about leaving Jonathan home in England. She said she thought he should come, but they should ask him what he wanted. They brought Jonathan into their conversation. He said that he wanted to go with them, no matter what. "I want a chance at a new life, just like the others," he said. "Please don't leave me here. I want to choose how I serve God. I want to be with Reverend

Mather, Reverend Denton, and my whole family. I can make it. I know I can." The look on his face told them he knew what he wanted.

"Of course, you'll come!" Susan said, throwing her arms around him.

"We just wanted to hear it from you." Matthew hugged him too, and they all walked back into the house.

Susan knew she really had her work cut out for her. She first called upon Sarah, who was fourteen, and Martha, who was twelve. She knew she could just tell them what to do, and they would get it done fast. It would also keep them in the house and busy.

"Girls," she began, "the first thing we will need are bags to pack all our clothing in. We need ten bags, one for each person. Here is a stack of burlap. Make one for each of us, with a drawstring closing at the top. We'll use rope for the drawstring. It's good and strong. Then cut out a piece of fabric in a contrasting color in the shape of each person's initial. Please use your judgment. Don't make bags with fancy flowers for the boys!" (The girls giggled.)

"For Susan and Sarah, please put two letters . . . 'Su' and 'Sa.' For my bag, you can put 'Mom.' For Martha and Matthew, put 'Ma and Mt.' Sort these fabrics first, pinning them together, so you'll have what you need. We should end up with ten bags. Then make three or four bags with no initials. We'll decide later what we'll put in them . . . food, blankets, whatever. Work quickly and carefully. I've cut out one bag here, so you know the size. We have a lot more to do! And, girls, I'm making you responsible for seeing that all you children are fed breakfast and lunch. We all need to be strong and not hungry." Then Susan sent the girls off and called Jonathan.

"I need to ask you to keep an eye on the younger children for the next few days until we're packed and ready to go. Grab a few pots, take the children into the garden, and pick all the vegetables that are ripe or almost ripe." Jonathan began to speak, but Susan stopped him. "That's right—*everything*. Make a game out of it, so they don't get distracted. Use a different container for each vegetable. Abigail and I must go into the village to get other food. And if you see your father or David, send them to me right away. All set?"

Jonathan smiled and hugged his mother. "All set, Mom!" and he ran off.

Susan took a deep breath and went looking for Abigail. She was bringing in a basket of clothing that had been drying outside. They sat down on the porch steps while Susan explained what they were about to do.

"We're going into the village to see if we can buy rounds of hard cheese (maybe gouda), salted or smoked fish, salt, rye flour, and rice. Many barrels of water are brought on board, but I'm told that it becomes contaminated fairly quickly, so the crew drinks beer, and wine is used for cooking and drinking. We'll have to talk to your father about where to get beer and wine.

"Then, when we get home, we'll make a huge batch of

hardtack; that's a hard biscuit made from flour and water. It's baked for a long time. It's a staple food onboard ships. I'll show you how to do it, and you'll become an expert in one day!"

"Wow," said Abigail.

"This is the last family discussion we will have in this house." Matthew paused, looking around at the children. Then he took a breath and went on. "The house has been sold to the Jamisons, and I have arranged for safe transport for our whole family to Bristol, where those who are going will board the ship, *James*, for our trip to America. Even if you're not traveling, we invite you to see us off.  The others will get to wave goodbye.  We will pack our clothing and food tomorrow morning and depart tomorrow night once it is dark. You must say goodbye to your best friends—and *only* your best friends—tomorrow morning. Tell them you will write letters to them whenever there is a boat to bring mail back here. Your mother will help you with that.

"Do NOT—I repeat, do Not tell your friends you are going to America. That will be hard to do, I know, but for the safety of the family, you must not. They will no doubt guess, anyway, because they know we have been unhappy and worried.

"Before we depart, your mother will make us a delicious and special farewell dinner which we should enjoy. We should be thankful to God for all that we have had while living in this house. Thank you for all your help this past week preparing for this departure. And remember, we will journey together, so you don't have to worry! Now, head out and play for a while!"

No one made a sound. They all got up and walked quietly out of the house. Matthew's hands were red and sweaty when Susan took them in her hands and led him to the chairs by the fire. She poured each of them a mug of red wine, and they sat for a time, quietly talking and sipping.

"I hope we've thought of everything," Matthew said.

"I'm sure we haven't," said Susan with a chuckle. "Whatever we've forgotten doesn't matter. And those carts, by the way, look just as uncomfortable as you predicted!"

Matthew laughed. "They sure do! I'm just glad they fit in the barn so they can't be seen. By the way, the leather pouches you made for me to carry money under my breeches are great."

"I'm glad you like them," said Susan. "I also made a lot of pockets on the insides of my skirts for my money and other valuable things. I don't feel comfortable leaving them in a house or on the ship."

Matthew nodded. "I agree," he said.

"What did you finally do about all your clients, all your business? I know you were worried about it."

Matthew sighed and sipped his wine. "I certainly have been worried. I worked many years to build up that business, and I hate to leave it. But I think I've done the right thing. Do you remember meeting Henry Davenport, who owns the woolen mill? I once brought him to dinner when

I was first looking for clients?" Susan nodded affirmatively. "Well, I've gotten to know him over the years and have found him to be an honest businessman and a good friend. I asked his advice. He wanted time to think it over. When we next spoke, he had a suggestion. He said if I entrust my complete client list to him, he will see that most of the listing is distributed to three or four of his trusted friends, who he knows will treat them respectfully. The top four clients, who are all very important, he will handle himself, seeing that they get what they need and understand what the Mitchells are doing and why I could not speak with them myself. So the deed is done. We're free and clear to skip town!

"Are you ready, Mrs. Mitchell?" he said loudly, kissing her cheeks.

Susan laughed and hugged him, but he could see there were a few tears on her cheeks. After all, they had been married more than fifteen years, and she loved their home. She poured them each a little more wine and said, "Well, I think we're entitled to sit here a little longer, remember the good times, and enjoy our wine!" And so they did.

Everyone was pretty quiet the following day, packing the bags the girls had made. Susan checked each bag and made sure they included only items of clothing absolutely needed. They didn't have much, and the warm winter clothing was the most important. This seemed odd to the children since it was now the first week in May, and the weather was warm.

"Barnacle" packed the boat David had carved for him, and Hannah had the soft little doll she slept with every night. Twelve-year-old Martha packed a notebook so she could write letters, and pens and crayons. David also packed several notebooks with pens. He knew he would be helping his father with the animals and thought he might have to make notes concerning how much food was being consumed. He also liked to draw and, although he had no idea what he would see, he wanted to be prepared.

The food Susan and Abigail had bought, along with the vegetables from the garden, were packed in two bags, including more than 100 hardtack biscuits they had made. Abigail was quite proud of their accomplishment. Susan made sure she set out whatever wooden buckets they had to go into the cart. They had been told that some buckets would be on board to use as a latrine, but she was sure there would not be enough.

Finally, for the cart they would be riding, Susan loaded whatever blankets they had in the house. She was sure they would do some sleeping on the way to the ship, and they would be needed. Even if they couldn't take them aboard, at least they would be a little more comfortable getting there.

But now, there was little time, and they must have their final, celebratory dinner. Abigail and Sarah helped her in the kitchen. They set the table, brought out candles, and helped Susan prepare the food. The boys and Matthew built a fire to cook the meal and warm the room. They made sure the outside areas of the home were cleaned up for the next inhabitants. All the tools were put away in the shed, animals were fed, and kids cleaned up for dinner.

The table was ablaze with candlelight when Susan called them in to eat. They all sat down in silence. Matthew led them in a prayer of thanksgiving and hope, asking God to bless them on their journey and bring them all safely to America. Amen!

There was lots of chattering among the children as they ate the delicious meal. Many questions were asked that couldn't be answered, and some that could. In the end, Susan announced that they should all settle down with a blanket and try to get some sleep before Stephen arrived with his drivers. The older children cleaned up the dishes, wiped off the table, and packed the remains of the food while the younger children scurried off to their blankets. Susan knew that they were all so excited that they would do little sleeping. David and Matthew banked the fire so it would just leave embers by morning.

It was a clear, warm night with stars filling the sky and no moon. About midnight, Stephen and four other men arrived and quietly dismounted. Matthew met them by the door of the large barn. They spoke in whispers.

"Ready?" asked Stephen.

"Ready!" replied Matthew.

Very quietly, they opened the barn doors. The men all entered the barn and slowly pulled the large wagon and the smaller one out to the drive leading to the road. Then they brought out six horses from the barn and hooked four to the large wagon and two to the smaller one.

Susan was standing in the doorway of their house. She whispered to David and the older girls, "Bring out all the bags and set them here. I'll find out where they want them." Hardly making a sound, the children passed their bags to the older boys by the door, and they, in turn, piled them near the larger wagon, as Susan instructed. Then they brought out the bags of food and several jugs of liquid, placing them nearby.  After that, Susan told David to bring all the children outside the house and have them sit quietly on the porch.

Matthew took David with him, and the two men went into the barn to bring out two kegs of beer and several barrels of wine, which they placed near the smaller wagon. Susan went over to him and whispered, "I think you should now go into the house and carefully check it from top to bottom. See if we've forgotten anything. When you're finished, I will make a final check and then blow out all candles. I'll close and lock the door."

Meanwhile, the other men were leading the children, one at a time, to the larger wagon and helping them aboard. The men were gentle with them, telling them to climb aboard, find a comfortable spot, settle down, and remain quiet.

Hannah, "Barnacle," and little Susan were frightened, and Hannah began to cry. Her mother picked her up and climbed aboard. Jonathan took Barnacle by the hand, and they climbed on together.

"It's so *dark*!" said Barnacle as they moved under the canvas top. "That's *good*," whispered Jonathan. "No one can see us. Let's sit over here on this blanket." Susan brought Hannah over to Jonathan and put her on his lap. "I'll be right back," she whispered.

Susan returned to lock up the house while the men secured everything else into the two wagons.

Three men plus Matthew climbed aboard the covered wagon and took up the reins. The other two men climbed aboard the smaller wagon. The contents of that wagon (bags, kegs, and jugs of wine) were covered with a tarp. Then they took up the reins.

The two wagons headed out to the road. "We're off!" said Matthew, a little too loudly.

"Hooray!" said Barnacle, much too loudly, just like his dad.

Everybody said, "Shhh," as they headed down the road.

Matthew looked back at the dark shape that was their beautiful house, and he was glad that it was too dark for anyone to see the tears running down his cheeks.

The wagons picked up speed as they got farther away from the populated area. The children began to get used to the sound of the horses' hooves. On through the night, they went, encountering no other travelers. Stephen wanted to keep up the pace so they could be as far away as possible from Halifax when dawn broke. Susan was very proud of how well-behaved all the children were. After several hours, she passed around some hardtack and a canteen of water for anyone who wanted it. No one wanted to eat, but nearly everyone took a gulp or two of water. The little ones dozed off with their heads on an older sibling's shoulder or lap, a blanket over them. There were, indeed, cushions on the benches, so it wasn't so bad. But then, this was only the first night.

In the morning, the sun and a light breeze cheered up the children. The horses turned into a grassy area by the side of the road and stopped. They could all talk normally to one another and look out at the countryside. Susan passed around portions of cheese and bread and water canteens to everyone.

"Stephen says we will stop here for a short time," announced Matthew, "so you can all relieve yourselves as needed. Abigail and Sarah will pass out the buckets so you can take turns. There is a stream nearby, so please wash your hands and face carefully and rinse the buckets. Then we'll get back in the wagon. Stephen wants to make as much time as possible on this first day. We will be stopping at an inn tonight."

There was rattling and chattering as everyone shook off sleep and creaking muscles. The men jumped down from their seats and walked around, rubbing their aching muscles. Susan walked over to Matthew and asked how the men thought things went during the night.

"Quite well," he said, "much to my surprise. It was very quiet. We did not see another single wagon. Perhaps we're still too far away from Bristol. There's such a big shipping business now in Bristol that I thought the roads would be full of wagons."

"Just be thankful for what we've got so far," said Susan. "Get some rest and food."

By the time an hour was out, they had all eaten, washed, and packed themselves back into the wagon. So far, so good. They traveled at a good speed for the rest of the day. The children played games, talked about the adventure, or tried to rest. They were optimistic because they would get to sleep at an inn that night.

It was still light out when they arrived. They were at the front of a large barn next to a stone building that had a sign on the front that read, "Monastery of the Flowers." They all got down from the wagon and waited quietly for the men to come over from the barn. Stephen got there first. "We're changing the horses tonight," he said. "I can pick these same horses up on my way back. We'll have fresh, rested horses for the next leg of the trip, so we should make good time. Just follow me inside."

Everyone crowded around the door, eager to see inside. It was pretty dark because there were just a few small windows. But they could see a hall with benches near the doors and then, down a few steps, a large, open dining room. Candles were on the tables, some of them lit. Several people sat at one table eating. The smell of meat cooking wafted through the room.

The children began speculating about what kind of meat it might be. A large fireplace took up one whole wall.

There were various cooking areas inside the fire area with large and small pots bubbling with food, some hanging from chains and others on iron stands.

"Just relax on these benches," said Stephen. "Someone will get you settled soon." He moved to a large desk in the corner and began talking to a man in a monk's robe. Matthew joined him. Soon, they all came over to where the children were seated.

"Welcome to our inn," said the man in the robe. "We will accommodate you as best we can and hope you will be comfortable. First, you may take a place at any table and eat lamb with potatoes and vegetables. Then we will show you where you'll sleep."

Susan led the children to tables and indicated where they should sit. The men also sat down and were immediately brought tankards of beer. Susan and Matthew sat with "Barnacle" and Hanna. Plates of food were served to all, along with a spoon. The food smelled wonderful and, according to the children, tasted wonderful too. The older children helped the younger ones cut the big pieces of meat, and Susan took care of Barnacle and Hanna. Small tankards of water were brought to each table.

David came over and asked if they were allowed to have a second portion, and Matthew said yes, as long as they asked politely, saying "please." David also asked if he could have a beer and, after thinking for a moment, Matthew said, "Yes, but only one. We have to keep sharp."

"You bet," said David with a smile.

When they had all finished eating, the monk led them up some stairs to a large room. Straw mattresses were lined up everywhere, with a blanket on each. The monk told them to roll up their coats or jackets to make a pillow for themselves. Susan and Matthew had a larger mattress together, and Susan told him she'd bring in a few extra blankets from the cart. The monk said that there were buckets outside, next to the barn, should they need to relieve themselves. He then left them on their own.

Full of good food and tired from the long ride, the children quickly fell asleep. Susan and Matthew found Barnacle and Hannah immediately joined them in their bed. Both children dropped right off to sleep. Susan and Matthew were not far behind them.

Stephen woke everyone up at sunrise. "We have to be on the road," he said. "We've got a long day ahead."

With the fresh horses, they took off at a good clip. On this day, they passed other wagons, all going in the opposite direction. The drivers all hailed each other but did not slow down. The children in Matthew's wagon remained quiet. They drove fast and quietly all day, not making a stop until late afternoon. It was a short stop by a brook so buckets  could be used and hands washed.

Stephen announced that they were making good time, and he wanted to continue throughout the night without stopping. "Don't worry," he said, "we'll stop at an inn tomorrow. The horses are still fresh, and I want to take advantage of that."

Susan told the children they should play some tag games that involved running around to have some exercise. Eventually, everyone was loaded back into the wagon, and they were off.

They did not see other wagons or horses until after it was dark. The moon was high, so the wagons were brightly lit. The children were frightened, so they kept quiet. Several wagons had stopped by the side of the road to rest, and the drivers stared at them as they went by. They ate some cold, cooked meat with cheese and bread which Susan had prepared, and drank some water. Anyone who needed to used a bucket as they rode along, which was quite uncomfortable but prompted some laughter and giggles from the children.

They stopped to rest and wash in the late morning. By afternoon, they were occasionally passing by farm houses and riding through small villages. They arrived at an inn after dark that was quite similar to the first one where they had stayed.

Again, the horses were exchanged for fresh ones, the wagons stored in the barn, and the family was served dinner inside by the fire. By then, the children were becoming veterans, remarking on the good weather they had experienced so far and commenting on how good the food was. David didn't have to ask permission for a mug of beer this time. He was assuming a leadership role by showing the children where they were to sleep. Susan and Matthew were exhausted but pleased.

Matthew decided to let David take his place for a day sitting up with the drivers "so he can get a feel for the wagons."

"Yes," agreed Susan, smiling, "and the children will be glad to have you back with them for a day."

Meanwhile, Stephen shared a beer and some conversation with men he knew from all his trips on this route. He wanted to find out if there were other families headed for ships and how dangerous Bristol would be.

Later, he reported to Matthew that they were the only large group in the Bristol area. However, there were still men questioning people at the inns and on the docks. "You should get on board your ship within a day or so of arriving," he said. The good news was that their ship, the *James*, was still in port. He would drop them at the inn, and when they were ready to board, he would put their bags on board, and they could walk to the ship in several small groups.

David liked riding up front with the men, especially enjoying their conversation. They taught him how the horses were handled and gave him a turn at the reins.

Without warning, they were suddenly entering a very densely forested area. It was dark in the dead of night. Stephen took hold of the reins from David and explained that they were entering a large forest and would not be on the other side for several hours.

"There are no signposts," said David, "and it's so black

out. How do you know where you're going?" He was happy to relinquish control of the horses.

Stephen laughed lightly. "There are no signposts anywhere on this road. We have just traveled them so often that we always know where we are. You're lucky to be riding with the experts, David!"

"Wow, I guess I am," said David with a smile.

It took two more full days and nights to reach Bristol. The closer they got, the busier the road became. Stephen decided to skip the final inn stop and push on to Bristol. It was around midnight when they finally arrived at the inn in Bristol. The horses were exhausted, as were all the people on board.

Matthew assembled his family by the door of the inn and said a prayer, thanking God for their safe arrival. The smaller children were grumbling and crying, and the older children were tired, hungry, and uncomfortable. Susan and Matthew remained outside while the family stepped inside, ate their meal, and headed to bed. No instructions were needed!

The following morning, Matthew was the first to wake up at dawn. He quietly woke up David, and the two of them dressed and quickly slipped out of the inn. Matthew wanted to get the lay of the land. There were a number of bars, inns, and shops along what they knew would be a bustling street by the middle of the day. The harbor lay straight ahead of them. They could see it was filled with the masts and furled sails of ships parked closely together, waiting to sail. There was only a slight wind, so the tops of the masts were bobbing only slightly to and fro.

"Let's get something to eat," said Matthew. He and David spied tables and chairs outside a bar on the cobblestone sidewalk. They grabbed two chairs at a table and sat down. When a waiter appeared, they ordered sliced ham, bread, and one mug of beer, which the two shared. Then they sat back, looked around, and started to talk.

"The first thing we have to do is find our ship," said David. "It's so crowded I don't think it will be easy."

"You're right," said Matthew. "When we finish eating, we'll start at one end of the docks and work our way as quickly as possible to the other end, looking for the name. I need to talk to the captain, and then we need to get everyone aboard."

"I hope to God it's still here," said David.

When the food arrived, they quickly ate some and put the rest in their pockets for later. They shared the beer as they watched the people rushing about the street.

Matthew suddenly said, "Okay, let's go!"

They left their chairs and moved quickly toward the harbor. Matthew had already given the waiter the money for their food.

As they rushed toward the canal at the end of the street, they could see buildings two and three stories high and nothing but ship masts in between. If only they could get to the end of these little streets to the wharf!

"We're almost there!" shouted Matthew as he reached the end.

David was confused and rattled by all the commotion—carts, horses, luggage on wagons, crowds of people—but he kept close behind his father. "I'm right with you, Dad!" he shouted.

When they both emerged on the wide street that ran along the canal edge, they stopped to catch their breath and look around. David had never seen so many ships before! And they all looked busy! Loading and unloading, people streaming on and off.

Matthew said, "Okay, the name of the ship is usually painted across the stern—that's the back of the boat." The boats were parked on either side of piers that stretched out into the water. "We'll each take one side of the pier. Start here and go all the way toward the end. Just look for the name 'James.' Give me a shout if you find it, and I will do the same to you."

It was only half an hour before David heard Matthew calling him and waving his arms in the air. He hurried ahead to where his father was standing.

There she was! And what a beautiful ship! It looked much bigger than what David had imagined. They nodded to each other and began examining the ship. It looked to be in excellent condition, with the mahogany well polished. The people walking around onboard looked to be a mixed bunch. Some were clearly seamen, strong, rough looking, in cotton shirts and wide pants. For the most part, they were carrying heavy boxes and luggage toward a large opening in the deck toward the stern. They dropped their load down the hole where other hands caught it and moved off into the darkness below.

Other people on board looked more ordinary, like themselves. In fact, Matthew said he recognized one of the men and was going aboard to talk to him about signing up with the captain. David said he would go with him, but he had difficulty hearing what Matthew was saying because the din of the crowd and the wharf was so loud. Matthew told him that was okay; just stick with him the whole time. David nodded, and they both went off toward the gangplank.

David said that night that he would never forget his first time on a ship. It was exciting but also fearsome. He could feel the slight movement of the deck under his feet and wondered what it would be like with a big wind. His heart was pounding. Matthew had already connected with the man he knew who told them he only had a few minutes to talk because he had goods to deliver. Matthew introduced his elder son, and they shook hands. The man's name was John.

"I'm going to take you directly to the Reverend Mather. He can set the whole thing up for you, and I'm sure you can bring your family aboard tonight. God knows when we'll have a perfect wind; we've had a couple of false starts already. But it will give you time to settle in, and I'm quite sure you'll be a big help to Mather. Keep reminding him to change his disguise each day and keep your eyes out for those men called the Searchers. Get Mather out of the way before they spot him. Remember, until we're well out to sea, he's in jeopardy!" (*Until we're well out to sea*, thought Matthew, *we're ALL in jeopardy*!)

Once they were down below where the beds and galley were, they walked through the rows of bunks toward the stern of the ship, where a group of men was seated surrounding one man, the Reverend Mather. Introductions were made quickly and quietly. David stood close by and listened. Mather stood and shook hands with both Matthew and David. Then they all sat down on a bunk. John bid his farewells and left them so they could talk.

"Tell me about yourself and your family," Mather said to Matthew. For the next half hour, Matthew talked of his family, his successful business in Halifax, his religious upbringing, his close association with the Reverend Denton, and, most of all, his desire to have freedom of religion for himself and his whole family. He even told about Jonathan wanting to come to America so he could choose how best to serve God.

Mather expressed his sympathies for the family's struggles, his bravery in bringing them all on this perilous journey, and his hopes that they could work together to help bring the group safely to America. Matthew ended by saying he wanted to get his family aboard that very day. He was concerned about their safety.

Reverend Mather said that would be a good idea because

the ship would leave the minute the wind was right. "I will send the captain's mate to you right now so that he can sign you up. And I will say farewell for the moment so that I can protect my own safety! I'll see you all later. God be with you."

After signing on with the mate, Matthew and David hastened to the gangplank and were quickly down on the dock. Matthew took David's arm and told him they must get back to the inn right away to gather the family and their goods. "We're on our way!"

They needed Matthew's friends at the inn who brought them here to help lug all the supplies onto the ship. He told Susan to get the children a hearty meal at the inn while the men got everything aboard. The whole process took less than an hour. The children were very excited but did their best to behave and be helpful. Finally, they all met again together belowdecks, where the bunks were located. They were told which bunks were theirs. Susan told them to each put their bag on the bed to declare their ownership, which they did.

Because the winds were favorable the next day, the passengers wanted to weigh anchor and set sail. But the sailors insisted that they would not sail until all the goods were stowed and the hatches or the deck above cleared. So the passengers were forced to stow the items, which caused them grief because they had seen that another ship nearby, the *Diligence*, had sailed out of sight that morning. By the 27th of April, the wind was still from the west (the *wrong* direction), so a group of men, including Reverend Mather, went ashore to get more food and water for the animals. Matthew went with them, but David stayed on board.

The following evening, the winds had shifted, the *Diligence* had returned, and the *Angel Gabriel* (another ship, also bound for New England) had arrived.

Those aboard the *James* did not know that this trip to America would differ from most other trips in that events each day would be chronicled in a log kept by the Reverend Mather, who would publish it so the world could know their story. The weather, what fish were spied or caught, when Mather and the other minister on board (the Rev. Daniel Maud, father-in-law of Mrs. Mather), would say their daily prayers (called their "exercises"), even the days when the passengers were seasick. The log was lengthy and detailed.

**Rev. Richard Mather**

An important phase for all ships sailing out of England was the day of departure. "Departure" was not merely a matter of weighing anchor and sailing off for their destination. Since the wind had to be from a particular direction (east or south) to bring their square sails in position to take them west, it often took weeks to find themselves at sea finally. For example, Mather wrote that from the day they "lost sight of our old English coast until the 8th of August (when they reached land in America, in New Hampshire) was six weeks and five days (a total of forty-seven days), yet from the time the *James* first entered Kings Road (Bristol) on May 23rd until it finally arrived in Boston (where it was originally destined and went after being repaired) on August 7th, it was eighty-six days." So if one asks how long it took for the ship to get to America, the answer must be eighty-six days.

David was the first of the Mitchell family children to really gain his "sea legs" and not become seasick. This was due, no doubt, to the fact that he spent most of his day on deck. Other than helping to get the smaller children up and dressed in the morning, he could be found on deck, usually in the animal area. Within a few days, he was able to climb ladders, arms loaded with animal feed and supplies, steady as a rock. The first job he gave himself was to make a list of all the animals. He also listed what foods were available, what times of day they were fed, and how much food was available at the end of the day. Then he would go over the list with his father so they could keep track of how quickly the food was being consumed. He also checked the animal pens to be sure they were securely locked and made a few notes about the condition and behavior of the animals. Both Matthew and Reverend Mather appreciated this help.

David already knew there would be much to see each day, so he brought up his drawing materials from below and stowed them behind the stairs forward of the animal pens. They would be protected from wind and rain there, and he would be able to pull them out easily. He decided that for the first few days, he would just look at what went on.

*__May 27–30__ Matthew and some of the sailors had gone ashore; other sailor's were sent to buy more oats for the cattle, and bread and other provisions for the passengers coming back on board in the evening of the 30th.*

Meanwhile, down below, when the galley bell would ring, a member of each family would bring the food for their family to the cook, who would place it into a numbered net bag and put it into a cauldron of boiling water. When the cook decided the food was ready, each bag would be delivered to the table, where the family would transfer it to their family plates. (Given that all the dinner bags were cooked in one pot, the flavors and fragrances were no doubt shared, like it or not.)

The women passengers decided to handle the problem of seasickness among the children. They agreed that buckets should be provided to each family with one or more cases, and the buckets should be kept rinsed. Older children in any family were expected to be the helpers and assist passengers with no children. They also agreed that children should spend as much time as possible on deck, which would reduce the incidence of seasickness.

*__May 31__ The wind was from the east, but so many sailors were still away, and being it was Sunday, they could not depart. This was the second Sunday the Mitchells had been on board.*

*__June 1–2__ The wind was westerly and against them. Some of the company went ashore to wash linens and some to buy more hay and provisions. Toward night, the wind grew stronger, and many of the passengers became seasick.*

*__Thursday, June 4__ The wind was with them, the master and all the sailors being come aboard, we set sail and began the sea-voyage with glad hearts that God had loosed us from a long stay wherein we had been holden, and with hope and trust that he would graciously guide us to the end of the journey.*

This day we went about ten or twelve leagues before twelve o'clock, and then the wind turned to the west, and the tide also was at us; so we were forced to come to anchor again in the channel between Wales and Winnyard in Sommersett Shire, and there, we abode till about six or seven o'clock at night, and then the tide turning for us, we tacked about with the tide to and fro as the wind, and gained little yet continued all night till about two o'clock after midnight and then (the tide turning), we came to anchor again.

***Friday, June 5*** *The wind still strong at west; we tacked about again with the tide to and fro till about one o'clock after dinner, about which time the tide and wind being both against us, we came to anchor again within sight of Lundy, about two leagues short thereof. Lundy is an island about twenty leagues off the land's end and twenty-eight leagues from King's Road. This day, many passengers were very seasick and ill at ease through much vomiting.*

Matthew sent David below to check on the family because he knew most of them must be sick. Several of his children were ill, but only mildly. Susan had brought lemons, which she could purchase in town, and she was saving them to ward off scurvy. Susan said she had rationed the vegetables and fruits, so they were just now running out of them. A bigger problem was the blankets: virtually all linens were wet and soiled with vomit. The smell of vomit permeated the entire cabin. David said that Matthew suggested they get as many sick people as possible up on deck because they would feel better. Also, she and the other women should bring all the blankets on deck, rinse them in seawater, and hang them to dry. He would arrange to have some sailors assist them. Since the ship was anchored for the night, this would not present a problem.

Susan immediately gathered a group of other mothers and discussed it with them. She and David would help find sheltered places for the children to sit. The women decided to bring any dry clothing with them for the children.

It took awhile to get everything organized: older children supervising, well children caring for the sick ones. Actually, everyone who was well took care of the ill, whether an adult or child! Sailors helped find every possible sheltered area on the deck. A group of ten women worked with the sailors getting buckets of seawater to rinse the blankets. The fathers among the passengers helped by opening all the ports and the hatches down below so a brisk breeze could blow through and clear the air.

Actually, the laundering was not much of a washing, but at least the seawater got off the worst of the mess, although everything smelled of salt afterward.

**_June 5_** *The ship was unable to move for the next week due to the wind. This day at night, when the tide turned, we set sail again and so came on Saturday morning to anchor again, under Lundy, where we stayed because the wind was strong against us. Four of us were desirous to go ashore into the island; and speaking thereof to the master (the captain), he was very willing to satisfy us therein and went with us himself, Mr. Maude, Matthew Mitchell, Geo. Kendrick, myself, and some others accompanying him.*

*When we came into the island, we found only one house therein and walking in it from side to side, and end to end, one owner of the house being with us, we found thirty or forty head of cattle, about sixteen or twenty horses, and mares, goats, swine, geese, etc., and fowl and rabbits innumerable. The island is 1,700 acres of land but yields no corn. Here, we got some milk and fowl and cheese, which things my children were glad of, and so came aboard again; but the wind being strong against us, especially toward night, we rode there all night and the next day, and many of our passengers were by evening very sick.*

*__June 12__ A knight of the country dwelling near Hartford west, being aboard the Diligence, sent for me to come to speak with him. We had much wondering about what should be the matter, seeing I never knew him, nor he me. When I came to see him, he treated me courteously, invited me to his house, wished us all good successes, lamented the loss of them that stayed behind when so many of the best people for upholding religion were removed and taken away. The knight's name is Sir James Parret.*

*__Sunday, June 14__ The fourth Sabbath on ship-board. This day, Mr. Maud, Matthew Mitchell, and many of the passengers and of the Angel Gabriel's went to a church on shore called Nangle, where they heard two good and comfortable sermons made by an ancient, grave minister, whose name is Mr. Jessop*

## SIR JAMES PARRET

*__Monday morning, June 22__ The wind serving with a strong gale at east, we set sail from Milford Haven where we had waited for wind twelve days; and were carried forth with a speedy course; and about noon, lost all sight of land. The wind being strong, the sea was rough this day, and most of our passengers were very sick and ill through much casting.*

# GOD'S COUNTRY

This was the day (June 22) that would be counted as the first day at sea. From here on, the Reverend Mather would feel safe from the police. There would be no more landings until they arrived in America. He no longer thought he must don a disguise each day. He felt he could now concentrate on his work, his prayers, and his flock. This was the official Departure Day. Matthew Mitchell and his son had been taking care of all the animals and keeping track of their food, for which he was very grateful.

It was the passengers who were suffering most right now. The sea was rough, and all who were below were feeling the tossing of the ship worst. Water was leaking in through the hatch and soaking the bunks. The women tried to herd the children into dry areas and keep them there. The stench from vomiting was terrible, and many children remained quite ill. The adults and older children tied the younger ones to the masts to keep them from being injured. It would have helped if they could come up on deck, but finding a safe spot for all the women and children was not easy. Mothers found corners out of the way of the sailors and the sail lines.

**_Wednesday, June 23_** _The wind still easterly, and a very rainy day; we were carried forward apace and launched forth a great way into the deep; but people were still very sick. This day at evening, we lost sight of the three ships bound for New-fond-land, which had been in company with us from Kings Road, and the master thought it best for us to stay for the_ **Angel Gabriel**_, being bound for New-England as we were, rather than to leave her, and go with the other three. The_ **Angel Gabriel** _is a strong ship and well furnished with fourteen or sixteen pieces of ordnance, and, therefore, the seamen rather desired her company. Yet, she is slow in sailing, and therefore, we went sometimes with three sails less than we might have done, so we might not overgo her._

**_Thursday, June 24_** _The wind still easterly: in the morning, wet and rainy, but about noon, a faire sunshine day. Many of the passengers that had been sick before began to be far better and came with delight to walk above deck._

**_Monday morning, June 29_** _Wind still northerly; a faire cool day, at north and afterward more westward. This day, we saw many porpoises leaping and like about the ship. A faire, cool day. This morning about seven o'clock, a seaman struck a great porpoise and hauled it with ropes into the ship; for bignesses not much less than an hog of twenty or twenty-five shillings apiece . . . The seeing of him hauled into the ship . . . and opened upon the decks in view of all the company, was wonderful to us all, and marvelous merry sport and delightful to the women and children; so good was God unto us, in affording the day before spiritual refreshing_ *to our souls, and then a morning also of delightful recreation to our bodies, at the taking and opening of a huge and strange fish. In the afternoon, the Angel Gabriel sent their boat to our ship, to see how we did and took Master Captain Taylor aboard the Angel and Matthew Mitchell and me along with him. When we came there, we found the passengers who had been seasick now well*

*recovered the most of them; and two children who had the small pocks well recovered again. We were entreated to stay and sup there with their master, etc., and had good cheer, mutton boiled and roasted, roasted turkey, good sacke, etc. After loving and courteous entertainment, we took leave and came aboard the James again at night.*

**<u>Tuesday, June 30</u>** *A faire, hot summer day but small wind. This day we saw with wonder and delight an abundance of porpoises, and likewise some crampushes (whales?) as big as an ox, puffing and spewing up water as they went by the ship.*

**<u>Wednesday, July 1</u>** *A faire, hot summer day, but the wind westerly, so we gained little that day.*

**<u>Thursday, July 2</u>** *Rainy in the morning but in the afternoon, fair and clear, but little wind all day.*

**<u>Friday, July 3</u>** *Wind strong at southward. We were carried on apace; after eight or nine leagues, a watch as the seamen conceived. (A watch is four hours; a league is three miles.) This day some* *few of the weakest passengers had some small remembrance again of sea-qualms and sea-sickness.*

**_Saturday, July 4_** *A very strong wind, but not much for us. This day, the sea was very rough, and we saw the truth of scripture Psalm 107. Some were very seasick, but none could stand or go up on the deck because of the tossing and tumbling of the ship. This day, we lost sight of the Angel Gabriel, sailing slowly behind us, and we never saw her again any more.*

**_Monday, July 6_** *This morning, Matthew Mitchell and I spoke to the master captain desiring him that we might not stay for the Angel because we doubted the hay for the cattle would hold out, and many cases of water were leaked and spent: to witch request he gave free assent, and told the sailors to make all the sail they possibly could; and so we went as fast all day as the soft wind drove us.*

**_Wednesday, July 15_** *A strong wind, northerly, which made the sea rough, yet we went about eight or nine leagues a watch. Few of us were seasick, though. A wind not so strong and a sea not so rough would in the beginning of the journey have wrought more upon us; but now, we were better used to it.*

This day, both David and his father helped the passengers clean up their quarters and make them more livable. They opened as many portholes as they could, as well as the hatch, to let the brisk air blow through. Blankets were brought up on deck to dry. With the help of the sailors, buckets were washed with salt water and left in the air to dry. The women were able to prepare their net bags with food to be cooked for dinner. The sailors would prepare the fish.

**_Thursday, July 16_** *This day, we saw with wonder and delight an innumerable multitude of porpoises leaping and playing about the ship.*

**_Saturday, July 18_** *We saw this morning a great many of Bonnyetoes  leaping and playing about the ship. Bonneytoe is a fish somewhat bigger than a cod but less than a porpoise.*

**_Tuesday, July 21_** *In the morning, a great calm after a hot night. This morning, seamen took a Bonneytoe and opened him upon the deck which, after being cleaned and dressed, the captain sent Matthew Mitchell and me part, as good a fish in eating as good be desired. About noon, the wind became northeast, so in the afternoon, we went nine or ten leagues a watch.*

**_Thursday, July 23_** *A fine gale of wind at north by east. Toward evening, the seamen decided we were near to some land because the color of the water was changed; but sounding with a line of a hundred and sixty fathoms, they could find no bottom. It was a very cold wind, like as if it had been winter, which made some wish for more clothes.*

**_Friday, July 24_** *Wind still northerly but very faint. It was a great foggy mist and exceedingly cold as it had been December.*

*One would have wondered to have seen the innumerable numbers of fo wl which we saw swimming on every side of the ship, and mighty fishes rolling and tumbling in the water, twice as long and big as an ox. In the afternoon, we saw mighty whales spewing up water in the air like the smoke of a chimney and making the sea about them white and hoary as it is said in Job (xli. 32) of such incredible bigness that I will never wonder that the body of Jonas could be in the belly of a whale. At evening, the seamen sounded and found ground at fifty fathoms. On Friday in the evening, we had an hour or two of marvelous delightful recreation, which also was a feast unto us for many days after, while we fed upon the flesh of three huge porpoises, as well as many fat hogs striked by the seamen and hauled with ropes into the ship; the flesh of it was good meat with salt, pepper, and vinegar, the fat like bacon and the lean like bull-beef.*

**<u>Saturday, July 25</u>** *Saturday morning, they sounded again and found no bottom, deciding thereby that the day before when they found ground, they were on New-fond-land Bank on the end of it nearer to New England. This day, Matthew Mitchell and I, taking notice that the hay and water were scarce, went to the master, asking him to tell us how far it was to the journey's end so we might better know how to order water and provisions for the cattle which were all alive and in good liking. He conceived 250 leagues remained unfinished.*

**<u>Sunday, July 25</u>** *The fifth Sabbath from Milford haven and the tenth on ship-board, a faire sunshine summer day, and would* *have been very hot had not God allayed the heat with a good gale of southerly wind, by which we were carried on at seven leagues a watch. In the afternoon, the wind grew stronger, and it was a rough night for wind and rain, and some had beds all wet with rain leaking in through the sides of the ship.*

Matthew sent David below to check on the women and children. He found them struggling to block the leaks in the side of the ship and find themselves dry corners to hide themselves. The little children were crying and were very fearful while their mothers were frantically trying to protect them. David asked a few sailors if there was some extra sail they could use to block the leaks. They led him to a sail locker that contained torn sails that the passengers could use. The women immediately set to work emptying the sail locker and then set it up as a dry area for children. The locker was dry only because it was amidship with no parts of it contiguous with any outer wall of the ship.

**<u>Monday, July 27</u>** *The wind was still strong from the south. This day, we spent much time filling tons of empty casks with salt water, which was needed because much beer, fresh water, beef, and other provisions being spent, the ship went not so well, being too light for want of ballast.*

To provide ballast, sailors rolled all the empty casks on the upper decks over to the big hatch openings and lowered to men below, who would stow them in the deepest parts of the hull below the waterline.

"How do you get the water in the casks?" David asked one of the sailors.

"Just watch," he answered. Since siphons had not yet been invented, they likely used a method similar to this: Well below the waterline was a niche in the side of the hull built in the general shape of the cask. The sailor first pulled the cork out of the top of the empty cask. He then pulled a tube out of his pocket that looked like he had carved it out of whalebone (or a walrus tusk) and pushed one end into that hole. Then he pushed the cask into the niche. Finally, he pulled a small board on the ship's hull open just a little way, revealing a hole in the side of the ship. Then, quickly, he pushed the other end of the whalebone pipe into that hole. Water began immediately to pour into the whalebone pipe.

The cask filled up quickly, and the sailor slammed the board back in so the hole was closed. He then put the cork tightly back on the barrel and rolled it out of the way, where another sailor moved it into position for storage.

David could not believe his eyes. He had never seen anything like this before! "How does that work?!" he shouted.

The sailor smiled and said his captain had figured it out and he would explain later. For now, David should bring him another cask. All afternoon, David did nothing but roll barrels into position to be filled. The sailor worked efficiently to get them filled so several other sailors could stack them, neatly filling the empty space in the hull. David could not wait to return to his father to tell of his wonderful adventure.

*When this work was done, we set forth more sail and went till evening and all the night following with good speed on the journey.*

**_Tuesday, July 28_** *Great calm and very hot all morning: people and cattle were much afflicted with faintness, sweating, and heat. But thanks to the goodness of God, about noon, the wind blew at north and by east, which took us out of the heat and helped us forward on our way.*

*This afternoon, there came and lighted upon the ship a little land-bird with blue-colored feathers about the bigness of a sparrow, by which some conceived we were not far from land.*

**_Wednesday, July 29_** *Not extremely hot but a good gale of cooling wind. But since it was by north and west, it was against us, so we were forced to tack northward and southward and gained little.*

**_Thursday, July 30_** *A great foggy mist all forenoon, and the wind was against us. In the afternoon, the mist vanished, and the day cleared up, but the wind was still against us.*

**_Friday, July 31_** *A great foggy mist all forenoon, and the wind went north-west, which was against us. In the afternoon, the mist vanished, and the day cleared up, but the wind was still against us so that we gained little, being forced to run by course, viz., north and by east, and at night to run southward.*

*Saturday morning A cool wind at north, whereby we went on in course an hour or two, though very slowly because of the weakness of the wind. Afterward, it became a great calm; and the seamen sounded about one o'clock and found ground at sixty fathoms.*

*Presently after, another little land-bird came to light upon the sails of the ship.*

**<u>Sunday, August 2</u>** *The wind blew with a cool and comfortable gale at south all day, which carried us away with great speed toward our journey's end. So good was our loving God unto us as always, so also this day. Mr. Maud was exercised in the forenoon and I in the afternoon.*

**<u>Monday, August 3</u>** *But lest we should grow secure and neglect the Lord through an abundance of prosperity, the wise and loving God was pleased on Monday morning about three o'clock when we were upon the coast of land, to exercise us with a sore storm and tempest of wind and rain so that many of us passengers with wind and rain were raised out of beds, and seamen were forced to let down all the sails: and the ship was so tossed with fearful mountains and valleys of water as if we should have been overwhelmed and swallowed up. But it lasted not long: for at the poor prayers, the Lord was pleased to magnify his mercy in assuaging the winds and seas again about sun-rising. But the wind was becoming west against us. We floated upon the coast, making no dispatch of way all day and the night following; and besides, there was a great fog and mist all day, so we could not see to make land, but kept in all sail, and lay still, rather losing than gaining, but taking abundance of cod and halibut wherewith our bodies were abundantly refreshed after they had been tossed with the storm.*

**_Tuesday, August 4_** _The fog still continued all forenoon. About noon, the day cleared up, and the wind blew with a soft gale at south, and we set sail again, going on course, though very slowly because of the smallness of the wind. At night, it was calm and an abundance of rain._

**_Wednesday, August 5_** _Wednesday morning, we had a little wind at north, but a foggy forenoon. In the afternoon, the day somewhat cleared, but it became calm again. Thus, the Lord was pleased with foggy mists and want of winds to exercise patience and waiting upon his good leisure, still keeping us from sight of land, when the seamen believed us to be upon the coast. This day in the afternoon, we saw multitudes of great whales, which, by now, had grown ordinary and usual to behold._

**_Thursday, August 6_** _A foggy morning, afterward, a very hot day and great calm so we could make no way but lay still floating upon the coast and could not come to any sight of land._

**_Friday, August 7_** _A great fog, still; and a slender, soft wind at west south-west. In the afternoon, the wind weakened, and we went forward with good speed, though too far northward because the wind was so much on the west._

**_Saturday, August 8_** _We had a good gale of wind at west south-west; and this morning, the seamen took an abundance of mackrell, and about eight o'clock, we all had a clear and comfortable sight of America and made land again at an island called Menhiggin, an island without inhabitants about thirty-nine leagues northward_ *or north-east short of Cape Anne. A little from the island, we saw more northward, divers other islands called St. George Islands, and the maine land of northward and eastward as we sailed. This mercy of God we had cause more highly to esteem of because when we first saw land this morning, there was a great fog; and afterward, when the day cleared up, we saw many rocks and islands almost on every side of us, as Menhiggin, St. George Banks, Pemmequid, etc. Yet, in the midst of these dangers, God preserved us, though because of the thick fog, we could not see far about us to look unto ourselves. In the afternoon, the wind continuing still westward against us, we lay off again to the sea southward, and the seamen and many passengers delighted themselves in taking an abundance of mackrell.*

***Sunday, August 9*** *The seventh Sabbath from Milford and the twelfth on shipboard (eighty-fourth day onboard). This day was faire, clear, and comfortable, though the wind was directly against us, so we were forced to take too  and again southward and northward, gaining little, but were all day still in sight of land. Mr. Maud in the forenoon; I in the afternoon.*

***Monday, August 10*** *Monday morning, the wind still continuing against us, we came to anchor at Richmonds Island, in the east part of N.E., the bay of Massachusetts, where we were bound lying thirty leagues distant from us to the west. The seamen were willing here to cast anchor, partly because the wind was against us and partly because of necessity they must come to anchor to take in a pilot somewhere before we come to the bay, by reason* *the pilot knew the harbors no further but to the Ile of Shoales. When we came within sight of the island, the planters there being but two families and about forty persons were sore afraid of us; doubting lest we had been French come to pillage the island, as Penobscots had been served by them about ten days before. When we had come to anchor, and their fear was past, they came some of them aboard to us in shallops, and we went some of us ashore into the island to look for fresh water and grass for the cattle; and the planters bid us welcome and gave some of us courteous entertainment in their houses.*

**Tuesday, August 11** *Tuesday, we lay still at anchor at Richmonds Island, the wind being still against us.*

**Wednesday, August 12** *Wednesday morning, the wind serving with a fresh gale at north and by east, we set sail from Richmonds Island for Massachusetts Bay and went along the coast by Cape Porpus still within sight of land. This day, the wind was soft and gentle, and as we went along, the seamen and passengers took abundance of mackrell. Toward night, it became calm, so that then we could go very little way.*

**Thursday, August 13** *Thursday morning, the wind was against us at south-southwest, and so had been all night before, so we tacked to and fro, gaining little; but continuing on the coast toward Cape Anne and thirteen or fourteen leagues from the Ile of Richmond, but the wind being strong at south-southwest, they could not attain the purpose, and so were forced to lie off again to sea all night.*

**_Friday, August 14_** *Friday morning, the wind was strong at south-southwest, and so continued till toward evening, and then was somewhat milder. This day, we tacked to and again, all day, one while west and by north toward Iles of Shoales and another while-southeast to sea again; Cape Anne, whither or way was, lying from us south-southwest directly in the eye of the wind, so we could not come near into it. But in the evening by moonlight about ten o'clock, we came to anchor at Iles of Shoales, which are seven or eight islands and other great rocks, and there slept sweetly the night till break of day.*

**_Saturday, August 15_** *But the Lord had not done with us, not yet had let us see all his power and goodness which he would have us to take knowledge of; and therefore on Saturday morning about break of day, the Lord sent forth a most terrible storm of rain and easterly wind, whereby we were in as much danger as I think ever people were: for we lost in the morning three great anchors and cables of which cables, one having cost 50L never had been in any water before, two were broken by the violence of the waves, and the third cut by the seamen in extremity and distress to save the ship and their lives. And without cables and anchors were all lost, we had no outward means of deliverance but by losing sail, if so be we might get to sea from among the islands and rocks where we anchored: but the Lord let us see that the sails could not save us neither, no more than the cables and anchors; for by the force of the wind and rain, the sails were rent in sunder and split in pieces, as if they had been but rotten rags, so that of the foresail and sprisslesail there was scarce left so much* *as a handbreadth that was not rent in pieces and blown away into the sea. So that at the time, all hope that we should be saved in regard to any outward appearance was utterly taken away, and rather because we seemed to drive with full force of wind and rain directly upon a mighty rock standing out in sight above the water, so we did but continually wait, when we should hear and feel the doleful rushing and crushing of the ship upon the rock.*

*In the extremity and appearance of death, as distress and distraction would suffer us, we cried unto the Lord, and he was pleased to have compassion and pity upon us; for by his overruling providence and his own immediate good hand, he guided the ship past the rock, assuaged the violence of the sea and the wind and rain, and gave us a little respite to fit the ship with other sails, and sent us a fresh gale of wind by which we went on the day in a course southwest and west toward Cape Anne. [Editor's note: They were most likely in the eye of the storm at that time.] It was a day much to be remembered because, on this day, the Lord granted us as wonderful a deliverance as I think ever people had, out of as apparent danger as I think ever people felt. I am sure the seamen confessed they never knew the like. The Lord so imprinted the memory of it on their hearts, that we may be better for it, and be more careful to please him and to walk uprightly before him as long as we live; and I hope we shall not forget the passages of the morning until our dying day.*

*In the storm, one Mr. Willet of New Plymouth, and other three men with him, having been turned out of all the havings at Penobscot about a fortnight before, and coming along with us in our ship from Richmonds Island, with his boat and goods made fast at the stern of our ship, lost his boat with all that was therein, the violence of the waves breaking the boat in pieces, and sinking the bottom of it into the bottom of the sea.*

*And Richard Becon lending his help to the seamen at the hauling of a cable, had the cable catched about his arm, whereby his arm was crushed in pieces, and his right hand pulled away, and himself brought into doleful and previous pain and misery.*

*But in all the grievous storm, my fear was less when I considered the clearness of my calling from God this way, and in some measure (the Lord's holy name be blessed for it), he gave us hearts contented and willing that he should do with us and ours what he pleased and what might be most for the glory of his name, and in what we rested ourselves. But when news was brought unto us into the gunrooms that the danger was past, oh, how our hearts did then relent and melt within us! And how we burst out into tears of joy amongst ourselves, in love unto the gracious God, and admiration of his kindness in granting to his poor servants such an extraordinary and miraculous deliverance. His holy name be blessed forever.*

**<u>Sunday, August 16</u>** *This day we went on sails toward Cape Anne, as the wind would suffer, and our poor sails allow, and came within sight thereof the other morning, which Sabbath being the thirteenth, we kept on ship-board, was a marvelous pleasant day, for a fresh gale of wind & clear sunshine weather. This day, we went directly before the wind and had delight all along the coast as we went, and came to anchor at low tide in the evening at Nantacot, in a most pleasant harbor, like to which I had never seen, amongst a great many islands on every side.*

*Now, the journey, by the goodness of God, was very prosperous unto
us in every manner of way. First of all, it was very safe and healthful
to us; for, though we were 100 passengers in the ship, besides twenty-
three seamen, and twenty-three cows and heyfers, three suckling calves
and eight mares, yet not one of all these died on the way, neither person
nor cattle, but came all alive to land, and many of the cattle in better
liking than when we first entered the ship; and most of the passengers
in as good health as ever, and none better than my own family and my
weak wife and little Joseph, as well as any other. Fevers, small pocks,
and such diseases as have afflicted other passengers the Lord kept from
among us and put upon us no grief in our bodies but a little seasickness
in the beginning of the voyage . . . We all had a comfortable variety of
food; for seeing we were not tied to the ship's diet of salt fish and salt
beef and the like, we had liberty to change for other food which might
sort better with health and stomaches; and therefore, sometimes, we
used bacon and buttered pease, sometimes, buttered bag-pudding made
with currents and raisins, and sometimes, drinks pottage of beer and
oatmeal, and sometimes, water pottage well buttered.*

*The second storm on the fifteenth was indeed very terrible and
grievous, insomuch that when we came to land, we found many mighty
trees rent in pieces, and others turned up by the roots by the fierceness;
and a barke going from the bay to Marvil head, with planters and
seamen aboard to the number of about twenty-three, was cast away
in the storm, and all the people therein perished, except one man and*

*his wife, that were spared to report the news. And the Angel Gabriel, being at anchor at Pemmaquid, was burst in pieces and cast away in the storm, and most of the cattle and other goods, with one seaman and three or four passengers, died along the way.*

# THE NEW COUNTRY

Once the ship had anchored in the harbor for several days, Matthew decided it was time to get things organized. The animals had been taken off the ship, and some of the crew, along with the captain, had disappeared into the streets of Boston.

The Mitchells were all still suffering from the effects of the storm, so they spent a good part of the day, along with the other passengers, sitting quietly, staring at the city. There were many buildings, most of them one or two stories high, including a church, small houses where people resided, and a strip of warehouses with shops and restaurants on the first floor. There were nearly 1,000 people in Boston at that time. Building had begun on what would be the Boston Latin School, and Harvard College would be finished within a year. People were milling in every direction, carrying parcels and boxes. In the street were horses pulling carts and cows wandering by themselves.

Their ship was anchored too far away from shore to hear sounds, but they could also see other ships, like their own, nearby. Matthew sat talking quietly with Susan.

"I've not been able to find anyone who knows anything about where we're going to live," he said, "but we'd better find out soon because the weather won't stay warm forever. This town is hopping with new people, and they all have to have a place to live. Samuel will join us shortly. He and I will go ashore to explore. But, first, we need a decent, dry place to sleep, good food, and lots of it, and a place to wash ourselves and absolutely everything we own. We're a mess!"

"But we're alive!" shouted Susan, throwing her arms around his neck.

"Yea!" shouted the children. "We made it!"

"We made it," echoed Susan. Then she started to cry because she was just too tired to do anything else. Susan wrapped her in her arms and kissed her pink cheeks over and over. The rest of the children cheered and yelled and clapped their hands. David shook his father's hand and then hugged him enthusiastically. "You were great, Dad!" he said.

"So were you, son," Matthew returned with a smile. "We made a great team."

Just then, Samuel came around the forward cabin and joined them. "Well," he said cheerily, "sounds like you're happy with your newfound home!" Matthew jumped up and shook his hand. "Pull up a wet cushion and join us," he said.

Samuel smiled and said, "I'm just itching to get ashore.

We'd better get busy and find us a place to live, Matthew. Are you ready?"

"As ready as I'll ever be," said Matthew with a sigh. Pushing himself to his feet, he turned to Susan and said, "Don't worry, Susan. I checked all my money and valuables, and everything is in good order. Nothing lost. Be sure to check your little bank. We won't have to count on that 'up-front' money we gave when we came on board. I didn't really trust the plan the captain gave me. I think the company people are all a bunch of crooks like Reverend Denton told us last year. I have plenty for land and a house. It's just a matter of finding it. This town looks very crowded, and winter is moving in. But we'll see! I'll have us off here by tomorrow. While we're gone, you might put your things together as best you can."

The two men climbed down a rope ladder to the shallop that Samuel had arranged for. A shallop was a rowboat that was convenient for ferrying people and belongings to shore. The children all waved, but in no time, the shallop was out of sight; mere specks headed for shore.

After a full day of walking the streets, examining buildings, and talking to men in shops, they stopped in a pub for a beer and something to eat. They were exhausted.

"I couldn't believe what the captain told us," Matthew exclaimed. They had encountered Captain Taylor on one of the piers and pressed him for information about their accommodations. Finally, after both men pressured him for information, Taylor pulled out a drawing of land plots and showed it to Samuel and Matthew. Their names were on two lots of about five acres each. They were very poor lots with no water nearby, located in a remote part of the city. When they pressed Taylor for information, he dodged their questions and then moved off down the street, leaving them with the drawing.

Matthew sighed.

"He was great as a sea captain," Samuel said, "but a real crook when it came to making a business deal. He stole our money! This land he's showing us is useless! You couldn't grow poison on that! And it is dry and hard as a rock! And how could we build a house on it before winter?"

"Well, I'm not surprised," said Matthew, "but what do we do now?"

Samuel continued, "The only other houses we've seen are holes in the ground with thatch roofs."

"I know," said Matthew. "I've seen houses like that in Holland. The Dutch built them in the countryside that hasn't been settled. They are quite clever, actually. When you have a short time to build a shelter and get plants in the ground, you first dig a hole one story deep, a big square the size of one room. Then on one side of it, you build a fireplace for heat and cooking. The chimney sticks up above ground level.

"While you're doing that, other members of the family or neighbors willing to help start clearing the surrounding land to ready it for planting. If you have money, you might be able to hire extra people to work on it. Next, you have to collect wood and thatch to make a roof. A hole in the roof allows the chimney to come through. God willing, all the work is done, and a late crop of winter vegetables is planted before the really cold weather moves in. It isn't easy, and it's not my choice for solving our problem. Too many people in one room and not enough time!"

Samuel was discouraged. The two men entered a tavern and sat silently, eating bread and sipping beer. "If only we'd arrived a few months earlier," he said. "Those people brought builders with them. They were able to build pretty sturdy houses. They also brought tools from England, and they knew what to do. You know, the larger houses made from trees? That's what we need."

Matthew was thinking, so he said nothing for a few minutes. Then he put down his spoon and took a good gulp of beer. "Samuel, you are absolutely right!" he said. "Only we can't build it ourselves. We need one that's already been built! One with a thick thatched roof and a good fireplace. One room is enough as long as it's big enough for all of us. It won't be fancy, but it will get us through the winter."

Now Matthew was getting excited. If they needed a few helpers to fix it up, they'd hire them. All they had to do was find such a place! One whose owners had or would move out. It might cost a pretty penny, but at least they'd make it through the winter.

"Here's what we'll do: I'll arrange for us all to stay at an inn for two weeks, longer if necessary, while we find a place. We'll eat there and sleep there. What do you say?"

Samuel was dumbfounded. He knew Matthew was a smart merchant and had many good ideas at town meetings, but this was amazing. Could they do it? *Well,* he thought, *I can't think of a better idea, and time is short.* "Let's do it!" he exclaimed, reaching for a handshake from Matthew. Matthew had a big smile as he shook Samuel's hand enthusiastically. "I'll share the cost with you," said Samuel.

They finished eating and started on their quest immediately by talking to the owner of the pub they were in. He did not know of any available houses but sent them to a large inn he knew of at the city's edge. "They might have room enough for you all there."

It was dark out by the time both men headed back to the ship to fill their families in on their ideas. They were exhausted. The children and any other adults around listened with rapt attention. All the families left on the ship faced the same task: finding a place to live. Matthew said he and Samuel would set out early the following day to search for an inn to stay in until they had found a house. The children would all be given tasks to help with the process. In the meantime, they should get a good night's sleep.

They were all up early in the morning to wish good luck to Matthew and Samuel, and they waved goodbye to the men as they headed to shore in the shallop.

They did not have difficulty finding the inn. The owner of the tavern had given good directions. It was large, indeed, like the inns they encountered on the road from Bristol. They entered and quickly found the owner. Matthew told him there were eleven of them, three adults and eight children. He estimated they'd need five or six beds, and they'd bring some blankets of their own. The owner said that was fine, but he'd need two weeks in advance, $50 a week, including food. Matthew said that would be satisfactory.

The three men toured the inn, checked the sleeping area upstairs, which was divided into separate but not really private sections, a washing area in the back of the kitchen, as well as a latrine.

Matthew took the money out of his pocket and handed it to the owner, Jake. The three men introduced themselves to each other and shook hands. Jake then invited them to have lunch "on the house," which they did because Matthew wanted to check the quality of the food. They decided it was good and went on their way. They had a lot of house hunting to do. He thanked Jake, and they left the inn.

Both Samuel and Matthew were strong, healthy men who knew how to build. But right now, they needed a finished home that would get the eleven members of their family through the winter. If the building was strong but needed repairs, that was all right. They knew they could find helpers who would be willing to work for money. They decided to each take a different route through the town and meet up again in several hours. They would visit taverns, inns, churches, and public buildings, talking to those they met. Someone, they figured, would be able to give them a lead. They agreed to meet back at the ship by dark.

When they did return, they were tired, hungry . . . and without a house. Fortunately, Susan had purchased some beef, vegetables, and potatoes in the town and cooked up a big stew. Everyone found a place to sit, the food was passed out, and the children began to pummel the men with questions.

Matthew began, "Well, to begin with," he said, "there are these villages of little Indian houses. And I do mean little! They are round and called Wetu. Looked like they would sleep about four people, very close together. The women build them down near the water for the summer growing months. Not suitable for winter at all.

"Then there are Colonial Villages that have what are called English Wigwams. They are a little larger than the Wetu and are covered with bark but have just one room with a small fireplace at one end. Roofs were covered with thatch. The Wetu could be made larger, but I didn't hear of any or see any. Again, they just won't work for our family. Samuel, how did you do? Did you see anything promising?"

"I didn't see much, but I heard of something quite interesting. I spoke with a man in a tavern who said the larger homes that colonists built were located a little out of town. What he described would be plenty big enough for our family.

"The men who built them had brought tools with them from England and nails and iron hardware. They built the house on plots that had enough farmland to raise whatever food they would require. The men cut down trees in the woods and then used axes to chop them from round to square. Finally, they fit the pieces together to make a frame."

"A house with a frame!" interrupted Matthew. "That's what we need."

"Yes," said Samuel. "Then they split more wood to make thin boards called clapboards which are nailed together over the frame of the house. The roof is made of thatch, but we know all about that." He said the house could be made as big as you want but would usually have just one room. "They are called Lean-to houses," Samuel said. "Although they are not as comfortable as what we had in England, they will work." Then he paused. "Unfortunately, no one I talked to knew of any empty or available houses of this type. Sorry." Several of the children groaned. Samuel stood up and moved to the stove to take another serving of stew.

"Well, don't worry," said Matthew cheerfully, "this was just our first day out! And we did find something you'll like! Until we get set up in a house, you'll be staying at an inn called the Londonderry. We'll take you there tomorrow. It will be very much like the inns we stayed at on the way here from Halifax. And the food is just as good. Samuel and I were treated to lunch there yesterday. How does that sound?"

The children clapped their hands and gave a cheer.

After the children went to bed and Samuel headed back to the other side of the ship where he was sleeping, Matthew sat with Susan and shared a tankard of beer.

"We just need to get through this winter," she began.

"Well," said Matthew, "I have a little bit of promising news: Do you remember when, some time ago, I told you Reverend Denton told me about a Mr. Pynchon who came from Springfield?"

"Oh yes," Susan responded. "He was also planning on taking his family to America, right?"

"Right. According to Reverend Denton, he is very knowledgeable about the quality of land for farming. He told me to contact him when we got here for help buying land for our house. But, unfortunately, he left five years ago for America, long before we did. God only knows where he is now. He is quite wealthy and is one of the heads of his father's Merchant Adventuring company. They want to start a business shipping animal skins home to England for sale. Apparently, the animals are quite plentiful, and the business is quite lucrative. I asked around a little today to see if anyone knows where he is but had no luck.

"What I have not told you before is that before we left England, I met with him and told him what we would be looking for. I asked if there was some way we could be part of the business he was hoping to start or buy into it. I told him I had money I could invest. He knew of my reputation as a merchant and was very receptive. He said he would be glad to include me and would sign any documents for me. I gave him enough money to convince him I was serious and said I would find him once we arrived in America."

"Do you think you can trust him?" asked Susan.

"Well," Matthew responded, "it's a long shot, but I figure a reasonable one. We'll see. First, I have to find him!"

Pynchon did indeed sail from Southampton in 1630 with his family and a family friend, Gov. John Winthrop. Since Pynchon was one of the wealthiest men in the company, he brought with him one or two maidservants and several manservants who could help build a house, farm the land, look after the cattle and horses, and sail a boat. Besides being responsible for seeing to his family affairs, Pynchon was in charge of buying guns and ammunition to defend the company's settlement.

It is from this point in Matthew's quest that you can best observe how these men, three of the most interesting and important colonial "adventurers" survived, pursued their goals, and settled what would become the state of Connecticut. No one was a close friend to the others, but they all had interests in common. They were basically the same age: Matthew and Pynchon were both born in 1590 and Winthrop in 1588. All three were capable merchants, administrators, and leaders. All had families, but Matthew had, far and away, the largest family.

Since Matthew had given up a thriving business in England, he would have to recreate his livelihood wherever he settled now, augmenting the funds he had brought with him. Mr. Pynchon was the lynchpin in his plans. The key was to find him.

After settling his family in at the Londonderry, Matthew and Samuel went hunting, Samuel for houses in adjoining neighborhoods like Roxbury and Concord. Matthew went hunting for Pynchon, this time down by the loading docks. He figured he would be shipping animal skins to London at some point, and he was right. He encountered a merchant who was receiving furs from Pynchon to ship out. He told Matthew Pynchon lived in Salem and gave him the address.

But Matthew discovered that the Pynchons lived in Salem for just a few weeks and then moved to a settlement called Roxbury, which is now part of Boston. Not long after this move, Pynchon's wife died a victim in an epidemic of scurvy, along with 200 other newly arrived colonists, leaving Pynchon with four young children.

One of the first things he did was purchase a boat which he was using to sail up and down the coast, buying furs from the English trading posts. The fur on the North American animals was usually at its best when they had grown their winter coats, so the late fall and early winter was the Indians' best hunting season. Now, his business was thriving.

Pynchon was glad to see Matthew when they met at his house, as he remembered when he had bought into the company. He was especially happy that the family had survived the perilous trip from Bristol. He wanted to know how he could be of help to him. Matthew explained their circumstances, saying they needed to move into a house that had already been built for the winter. He and his brother-in-law could do repairs but not build an entire house of wood.

The timing of their meeting could not have been better for William Pynchon. The Connecticut River had proved to be a lucrative place where most of the furs exported came from. He had recently gone up the Connecticut River with a small group of men looking for a place to establish a trading post and settlement. Pynchon invited Matthew to take his whole family up there in the spring, and he would build them a house. They would be among the first settlers. In the meantime, he could find Matthew an existing home for the winter that they might rent or buy. He should return to the inn where they all were staying, and Pynchon would let them know.

Matthew's heart was pounding. He could not believe his good luck. He met up with Samuel at the Londonderry and breathlessly told him his story. Samuel was delighted but warned him, as he had in the past, about the "company." "Remember that Pynchon may well be your friend, but the company's interests come first. But I'll back you up on everything, and I'll try to check out the truth of whatever he tells us.

"Right now, I'm starving. I haven't had anything to eat all day. Would you like to order?"

There were only a few people in the big dining room since it was well past the dinner hour. Matthew looked around the room, heaved a sigh, and said, "I don't think so. I've got one of those stones in my belly like I had last year, so I'm not feeling so well. I think I'll wait until tomorrow. It might pass."

Matthew sipped slowly on a beer while Samuel ate a hearty lamb stew. Then they went upstairs, where Susan was settling the children down for the night. Before letting the men tell of their adventures, she told them she had managed to find a laundry business nearby that was willing to take on the family's dirty clothes and blankets and slowly get them all washed and dried.

"It's costing quite a bit of money," she said, "but I felt it was worth it. Even if the whole family worked all day for weeks, we'd never get to the end of it. And if the weather suddenly turns cold, we're going to need those blankets! Anyway, the children are really exhausted. I don't want them getting sick. We've had enough of that."

The two men went back downstairs and settled themselves down on two chairs at a table near the open fire. They sat silently for a while, just resting and thinking back on their day while the fire flickered and the pots hissed. When Susan joined them, Samuel stood up and pulled over a third chair for her. She was not happy to hear about Matthew's "stone" and told him he must take some days to just rest.

"You have done nothing but push yourself since we climbed aboard the ship in Bristol," she said quietly. "You must drink lots of liquids, especially water if we can find it, and just pray it's a small one, like the last time . . . You were very lucky."

Matthew said he expected Pynchon would come through with a local house for them soon. Actually, it was sooner than any of them believed. Then, late in the afternoon of the following day, William Pynchon himself came looking for Matthew.

Jake, the inn's owner, found them a corner of the dining room that would afford them some privacy.

"Here's the story," Pynchon began. What followed was a long and detailed reporting of all his business deals since he left England, including a few negotiated while they were sailing. Pynchon seemed to relish his business successes. As his ship arrived in Salem, he negotiated with his friend, Governor Winthrop, a fellow passenger, for a place to stay until he had "situated" himself and his family.

Winthrop had been the leader of a self-governing Puritan group known as the Massachusetts Bay Colony. They had decided to come to America in 1620 because King Charles I of England was suppressing the religious practices of Puritans. Winthrop became governor of the Massachusetts Bay Colony and the founder of Boston.

After a few successful years, Mr. Pynchon turned his attention to the west, where most of the furs came from. In the summer of 1635 (the year Matthew and his family set sail for America), Mr. Pynchon took a small party up the Connecticut River to a place called Enfield Falls. Large, oceangoing ships could go no further than the bottom of the falls. They carried their shallops some distance above and beyond the falls to an Indian village called Agawam. There, they built their first house in the summer of 1635. Pynchon wanted to build a town at Agawam where he could bring his family, plant corn, raise cattle, and buy furs from the Indians.

The place would be called a plantation, and the men who built it would be called planters. The English built their first house in the summer of 1635.

Mr. Pynchon found the Mitchells a house in Concord, but it wasn't warm. The Mitchells could not have imagined a winter as difficult as they experienced that year. Susan kept saying it never gets this cold in England, nor the snow so deep. Every member of the family was ill for weeks, if not months. Fortunately, Susan could buy more wool to make warm clothes, especially for the little ones. They were all struggling with constant fevers and coughs and severe shortages of essential foods like fruits and vegetables. By the end of March, Matthew had reached the end of his rope.

"Let's get out of here," he told the family. "I've had enough."

Mr. Pynchon was also leaving, so they, along with a few other families, headed out with what supplies they could gather on the route Mr. Pynchon was taking to get to Agawam, or, as it was now being called, Springfield. Their house in Concord burned down shortly before they left, along with some of their possessions. They were very glad to get out. They began walking toward Agawam only one day after Mr. Pynchon and his group had set out.

Mr. Pynchon had, indeed, bought land and built the house he had promised, in Matthew's name, and so they had a home of their own when they arrived. They and seven other settlers signed the agreement.

But attacks by Indians quickly threatened all of them. Most of the signers stayed only a few months and then moved to other locations..The Mitchells were among those who moved on. They began walking toward Wethersfield only one day after Mr. Pynchon and his group set out.

The weather was perfect; sunny, with a light breeze. After several hours, they were passed by a group of four male Indians wo didn't stop but gave a friendly smile and greeting as they jogged by. In the late afternoon, the group passed several tents and signs of a campfire. While their group rested, Susan examined one tent carefully. An Indian woman approached her and smiled. "Do you wish to sleep in that tent tonight?" she asked in English. "Yes, we would," answered Susan, "but only if it is unoccupied. "Do you think it would be all right?"

"Yes it would," answered the Indian. "Those who slept there died of the plague. Their bones have been taken away for burial by their tribe. You should sweep out the tent before you sleep. In the morning, please burn the tent so no Indians will sleep in it and die,"

"We will be glad to do that" said Susan, and she extended her hand toward the Indian. The woman understood, smiled and extended her own hand in return. But Matthew suffered more losses by fire at the end of their first year in Agwam so he decided to return the land Pynchon sold him to the community and move his family to Springfield.

Unfortunately, he had no better luck there, where many of his cattle and goods were destroyed by Pequot Indians. In addition, the Indians killed several of his employees, including Samuel Butterfield, Matthew's son -in-law. This was a shattering event for the family and kept the colony, including the Mitchell family, in a constant state of alert and peril.

Again, Matthew moved the family, this time to Wethersfield, which proved to be more fortuitous. In addition to his large holdings of land and money in Wethersfield, Matthew also was known to have sound judgment and executive ability, which were recognized in the community. He was chosen a member of the General Court in 1637, and it was this court that declared war on the Pequots.

In April 1640, he was chosen recorder for Wethersfield, but the choice was rejected by the court, at the instigation of the ruling elder of the Wethersfield Church, Clement Chaplin, whose animosity toward Mitchell arose during church dissensions. Over the years, Matthew had never handled disputes among church members well or took them seriously enough. But thanks to the Reverend Mr. Denton, he had always managed to calm down disagreements.

This particular issue caused Mr. Mitchell, along with a major part of Denton's congregation, to move to Stamford. Chaplin's influence abated, however, when he was without the prestige of the General Court. So he sold out at Wethersfield and returned to England.

Life in Wethersfield, and then Stamford, became safer

and happier for the Mitchells than it ever had before. They lived in a large, beautiful house with a slate roof, glass windows, and a large, double fireplace. The older girls were thinking about attending college, and Jonathon said he would like to attend Harvard if it were possible.

Meanwhile, Susan was busy making clothing for the children when she could find fabric. But it seemed that Sarah was always missing, off somewhere just when she needed her. So she stopped David one day and asked him if he knew where she was.

"Gee, Mom, I don't know," he would reply. Then one day, he said, "Maybe she's off with someone. We're in a new place now, you know. Maybe she's made some new friends." Then he smiled and disappeared.

"Hmmm," said Susan. So the next time she saw Sarah, she asked her to walk down by the river with her. "I have something to talk to you about," she said. Once they sat down on a big tree log, Susan said, "I've been wondering if you have a boyfriend. I haven't seen any boys hovering around you, and I was just wondering if you have someone special these days."

Sarah immediately began to cry. Susan was consoling and put an arm around her. "It's okay, Sarah. I just wanted to know who it is and how you met him. That's all. Is he handsome?"

"Oh yes, Mom, he's *very* handsome! You can see him marching around with the militia. He's the head of our militia! Dad knows him."

"Oh, wow! Has he told you how beautiful you are?"

Sarah immediately began to cry again. "Mom, I love him! And he loves me. But I haven't told anyone until he formally asks me to marry him."

"Hmmm. I think it would be nice if he came to dinner at our house with all the kids from his house and your house so you can all get to know one another a little bit. Right? Would that be all right with you? Do you think he would like to come? And, by the way, what's his name?"

Sarah began to cry again, so Susan gave her a long hug and a kiss. "His name is Samuel Sherman," she blubbered. Susan pulled out a cloth to dry her eyes, and they both started to laugh. "Have you two been behaving yourselves? You know, if you haven't, they'll take you to the center of town and lock you in the stocks."

"Oh, I know all that. We've been good, don't worry."

"After the big dinner, Samuel will have to have an appointment with your father to discuss what a fine wife you'll be, right? After all, he's marrying the prettiest young lady in the whole town! Where is Samuel from?"

"He's from Essex. He came here with his parents last year. He's very smart."

"Yes, I'm sure he is," said Susan. "Now, don't you worry. I'll take care of everything."

Hugging her mother, Sarah ran off toward the village. When she arrived home, Susan found Matthew sitting on the porch.

"Did you see our little bride, Sarah?" she asked.

"She's not a bride, she's a child," Matthew replied.

"Not anymore," said Susan. She sat down next to her husband. "She's seventeen years old, almost eighteen. She and Samuel Sherman would like to get married. I told her she must have dinner first with all the children of both families, and he must then have a little meeting with you. How does that sound?"

"Oh, Sherman, eh? He's a fine young man. Have they gotten in any trouble?"

"Oh no," said Susan. "I told her if she did, they'd lock her in the stocks with her rear end in the air," she said with a smile. "She didn't like that idea. I'm going to make dinner for all the kids of both families, and then you can get together with Samuel and make sure his head's on straight. Okay?"

"Fine," said Matthew with a smile.

The dinner went fine . . . quite noisy but fine. Matthew's talk with Samuel was very serious, but successful. He had actually met Matthew before due to their work with the militia. He made sure Samuel understood that he would be the protector of his daughter for the rest of her life, especially against the Indians. He explained that he and Sarah's mother had shared a long and happy life, despite all the difficulties they've encountered.

"We've done it together!" he said emphatically. "That's why we've had love and happiness. So be sure you make your happiness together. Then your children will know they are  loved."

Then he and Samuel changed the subject and started talking about the latest tactics against the Pequots.

Susan was much more worried about finding fabric for a wedding dress than how to thwart the tribe. She was rescued by Samuel's mother, Grace, who was planning on moving to Stamford. "I've been down there several times," she said, "and there are a few merchants who carry fabrics. Let's try to figure out what you'll need, and then I'll see what I can find." They spent the whole afternoon plotting and scheming how many yards they would require and what colors would best suit Sarah. They traded stories about their children growing up and how challenging their new life is for them all.

Matthew, meanwhile, was suffering a lot of pain. He had a stone now that was clearly larger than the two he previously had. He knew he had to eat and drink lots of water, but it was difficult. But now, Susan wanted to introduce him to something new. A woman who was a friend of Grace's said that drinking spirits, but not too much, could really alleviate the pain. She gave Susan a large bottle and suggested she try it with Matthew.

One afternoon, she invited Matthew to walk down to the river with her just to talk and try a little spirits. He did not believe it would help but agreed to go. They sat for about half an hour, talking about the girls and the wedding and slowly sipping the spirits, which Matthew said had a good taste. Susan told Matthew to drink several ounces of the spirits when he really suffered from the pain. "Just sit on the porch for a while, and it will get better." And, for the most part, it did.

It seemed like no time had gone by until the wedding day. The Mitchell girls had gathered large piles of beautiful, fragrant flowers to decorate the church. When they finally opened the doors for the wedding, a rush of heady fragrance enveloped those entering the church. When everyone was seated, the Rev. Richard Denton entered and walked up the aisle. Matthew and Sarah followed him. Susan had made sure Matthew had a little spirits before he walked her down the aisle.

Samuel stood tall and handsome by the altar, his eyes glued on his bride. Sarah's gown was beautiful. Susan and Grace had chosen pale blue shades for the bodice, trimmed with tiny pearls and gems. The waistline had a taffeta sash that flowed to the hemline. Several petticoats of dark blue and white rustled slightly at her shoes when she walked. She wore a crown of white flowers in her hair.

They all emerged from the church and walked to the Mitchell house, which had been decorated by all the girls in the Sherman family for the party. Susan noticed that the Reverend Denton and Matthew spent quite a bit of time in close conversation on the porch. So she made a mental note to find out what they were talking about.

The Shermans owned a cabin near Stamford that Grace's cousin usually occupied, but right now, it was empty, so they invited the bride and groom to use it for a few weeks by themselves. Sarah and Samuel were very pleased by this generosity. Matthew had invited them to then live permanently at the Mitchell house since it was so large.

Everyone stood on the porch and waved good luck to the newlyweds as they rode off in a carriage.

Meanwhile, Stamford arose from the religious dilemma that confounded the Wethersfield community in 1640. If they all could not live in Christian harmony, then one faction of the conflict had to leave. Fortunately, suitable land, about   eighty miles away, purchased providentially from the Indians, was available.

The critical meeting in Wethersfield took place on Oct. 19, 1640, when twenty or thirty men pledged on forfeit of five pounds a man to begin the design of a plantation in a month. Mr. Richard Denton would move his family there by the sixteenth of May and the rest of the families by November. Every one of them had lived in Wethersfield and had participated in the creation of at least one town. Laying out the land and roads and charges for the lots was a very complex procedure. The doughty Matthew Mitchell and the young Francis Bell were delegated to lay out the new home lots. Five of the most respected figures, Denton, Mitchell, Ward, Rainer, and probably Coe, were chosen by ballots as townsmen and charged "to order the common affairs of the intended place and people . . ."

Then, one day, Matthew said he wanted to talk to as many family members as possible. Susan gathered everyone she could and told them to come to the porch and bring a cushion to sit on. The weather was perfect; warm but not hot, with a light breeze.  Many children from four or  five families came as well as about thirty adults.

Susan had told them that Matthew had a few important things he wanted to say.  Everyone was quiet.

"I've been sitting around here lately with nothing to do so I have decided to share with you some of my thoughts about some of the things that have happened to all of us. Some of the things were good!  Wonderful, in fact!  Others were and are terrible.  But we have to live with the good AND bad, so I've decided to throw both in the bucket."

# MATTHEW'S MESSAGE

*"I'd like to speak to you all about something that had an overwhelming influence on my life, your life and everyone's life and will continue to do so for possibly hundreds of years. It is a religious doctrine that was first started a century ago (during the 1500s) by Pope Alexander VI. Alexander was a Spaniard whose reign as pope was riddled with scandals related to his greed, corruption, and nepotism.*

*"This pope issued an order a year after explorer Christopher Columbus discovered (1492) what he called the Americas while on an expedition funded by the Spanish monarchy. Although this trip was meant to find a route to Asian trading centers, it also gave Spain a chance to expand both its own kingdom and Christianity's reach.*

*"While the pope's order (which was known as a Papal Bull) gave Spain permission to claim lands in this "New World," it also linked exploration and colonization to Christianity and conversion. Nations, it said, should ensure that the Catholic faith should be exalted. Non-Christians should be converted and barbarous nations should be overthrown.*

*"The pope's reasoning drew in part on an emerging concept*

called 'terra ellis', which is Latin for "empty land,"  Here's what it meant:  Any place not already occupied by Christians was considered free for the taking by Christians—regardless of how many people already live there or the advancement of their civilizations."

"Okay," said Matthew, "let's think about that for a minute: The concept of 'empty land' meant: where no-one could be seen living—where there were no towns and roads—where there were no Christian churches.  That is what this country we are now in looked like when ships full of colonists first arrived!  That concept could apply to this land.  No one had put up signs that read 'This big piece of empty land…these miles of meadows and mountains…are owned and are not for sale.  Likewise, no one on the ship alerted us.

"We could not assume that the people we encountered here were friends who would treat us with civility.  If we handed them a paper from the pope saying we had permission to build houses wherever we wished, they would not honor them.

'What is a Pope?' they might say.  After all, we could not even understand their language!  And they could not understand ours.  All this happened because, before we left, we were fed a dessert of lies!  It had to do with the concept of 'terra nulls', Latin for "Empty Land."  Any place not already occupied by Christian Europeans—regardless of how many people already lived there or the advancement of their civilization."

No wonder our houses were burned!  No wonder our cattle were stolen or killed!  Our Papal leaders had no respect for
the beliefs of the indians on the land.  Surely, the land <u>was</u>

*made by God.  The people living on the land had different beliefs about that ownership.*

*"Regardless of what the evil pope's decree said, we have struggled in many ways to make a good life here.  The price to my family—and I'm sure yours—has been high.  But things are improving; our families are growing, as are our farms.*

*"Perhaps someday the evil decree of an evil pope will be formally revoked by whoever is pope at that time and our school children will learn the story of their brave ancestors and the destructive legacy left by an evil Papal doctrine.  We must teach them the truth."*

Matthew had talked for a long time and he was tired.  His audience was silent for a minute or two but then applauded louder and stood up cheering.  They went over to him and slapped him on his back.  They all knew Matthew well and, like him, had given up a lot, lost relatives, and now were living in an oasis of calm and hope.

But now, he was spending most of his time in bed or on the porch, and she was quite out of ideas. The things that seemed to help him best were things like wild berry mix and hard apple cider and water. But he appeared to be declining over time, with body functions failing, and she was mostly spending time making him comfortable. Doctors had no treatments except surgery, which was invariably fatal. She had long talks with each of the children and asked them to spend time with him both on the porch and when they could just be with him in his room, helping to make him comfortable. She assured them it was okay to cry. She assured them how proud he was of each of them.

On the day Matthew died, the only one who didn't cry was Jonathon But he did have one special talk with his father. Matthew told him he had arranged for the Reverend Denton to take him to Harvard College for the next semester of schooling as soon as possible. Jonathon had just one more year of high school to complete, and Matthew felt that they could find a place for him to begin his studies early at the place he so wanted to be. Jonathon could not have been more grateful. He told his father he would work as hard as he could to be successful at the school. Then his father asked him to lie next to him for a while until he fell asleep. So Jonathon did, folding his father's hand in his.

One cold night, when Matthew finally passed away, the whole family was with him.

# A LOOK TO THE FUTURE:

Soon thereafter, as promised, the Rev. Denton travelled with Jonathon to Harvard College in Cambridge, staying with him there until he had settled  into his college studies.  As time went on, Jonathon became deeply interested in the study of theology.

After graduating from Harvard College, however, he preached his first sermon in Boston on June 24, 1649. Wherever he preached, his sermons were enthusiastically received,  Then, at the urgent request of Mr. Shepard,  he returned to Cambridge and preached there for the first time on August 12, 1649.

On the 20th of that month, Mr. Shepard died and the people unanimously invited Jonathon to become their pastor.  He accepted and was ordained on August 21, 1650. Some years later, he married Mrs. Margaret Shepard, the widow of his predecessor at Cambridge, "upon the general recommendation of that widow unto him," as Mather's Magnolia puts it.

They had four sons and two daughters.  The other two, Samuel and Jonathon, graduated from Harvard College.

Samuel is believed to have died unmarried.  Jonathan married Hannah Lynne, but was childless.  A daughter, Margaret, was married June 12, 1682, to Major Stephen Sewell of Salem, Mass. and was the mother of seventeen children.  Jonathon's descendants remain in this line.

David Mitchell, Matthew's older son, went to Stratford with his brother-in-law, the Honorable Samuel Sherman (a nephew of Roger Sherman, a signer of the Declaration of Independence) on February 26, 1656 and owned a house lot and considerable land.  At his death he was one of the largest proprietors in Stratford and quite prominent in the town as a land owner and farmer.  David had married Sarah, a daughter of Thomas Wheeler of Milford.  They had seven children; two of whom, Matthew and John, were the ancestors of most of those who carried the Mitchell name by the 1940s when the genealogy collection ended. Samuel Sherman died in 1884.  It is believed his wife died before him.

# BIBLIOGRAPHY

Armytage, F. and Tomlinson, J. *The Pynchons of Springfield, Founders and Colonizeers (1636-1702)*. Connecticut Valley Historical Museum, Springfield, Mass. 1969.

Bradford, William. *Of Plymouth Plantation.*, Zweihander Press, 2019.

*Journal of Richard Mather 1635, His Life and Death, 1670.* Paperback Classic Reprint Printed and Published by David Clapp, 9/1/12,

Boston 1990. Over 282 Washington St., Washington, D.C. 1850. Digitized by the Internet. Archive in 2014.

Connecticut Historical Society: *Records of the Particular Court of Connecticut, 1639-1663.* Hartford, 1928.

Fabend, Firth Haring: *A Dutch Family in the Middle Colonies 1660- 1800,* Rutgers University Press, New Brunswick and London, 1991.

Feinstein, Estelle F. *Stamford from Puritan to Patriot 1641-1774.* Stamford Bicentennial Corporation, 1976.

Innes, Stephen: *Labor in a New Land,* Princeton University Press, Princeton, N.J., 1983.

History by Majdalany, Jeanne; Genealogies by Wicks, Edith M. and Majdalany, Jeanne. *The Early Settlement of Stamford, Connecticut 1641-1700 including genealogies of the Stamford Families of the Seventeenth Century.* Heritage Books, Inc., Publishing Division, Westminster, Md. 1991.